LORD,
TEACH US YOUR
WAY

LORD,
TEACH US YOUR
WAY

MARGARET WHITE

authorHOUSE®

AuthorHouse™
1663 Liberty Drive
Bloomington, IN 47403
www.authorhouse.com
Phone: 1-800-839-8640

First published by AuthorHouse   12/09/2011

ISBN: 978-1-4678-7750-3 (sc)
ISBN: 978-1-4678-7751-0 (ebk)

Printed in the United States of America

Any people depicted in stock imagery provided by Thinkstock are models, and such images are being used for illustrative purposes only.
Certain stock imagery © Thinkstock.

This book is printed on acid-free paper.

Contents

Preface xi

CHAPTER 1
Discipleship 1

CHAPTER 2
The beatitudes 12

CHAPTER 3
The salt of the earth 68

CHAPTER 4
The light of the world 81

CHAPTER 5
The Law and the Prophets 89

CHAPTER 6
The Law of the Spirit 110

CHAPTER 7
Almsgiving 127

CHAPTER 8

Prayers and fasting.. 130

CHAPTER 9

No one can serve two masters.. 177

CHAPTER 10

Judgement and condemnation 182

CHAPTER 11

Cast not your pearls before the swine........................... 195

CHAPTER 12

Ask, seek and knock.. 199

CHAPTER 13

Love for others... 204

CHAPTER 14

Entering in at the strait gate... 207

CHAPTER 15

Building on the Rock... 228

This book is dedicated to disciples of the
LORD JESUS CHRIST

Preface

This book is based on the teachings of the Lord Jesus Christ to His followers, right at the beginning of His ministry. Of the messages that the Lord taught, this is one of the longest. In the gospel according to Matthew, it is recorded in three chapters: 5, 6, and 7.

These teachings are the foundation in a disciple's life. Therefore, we mustn't, at any point, ever think that they are too hard. The people to whom the Lord gave the teachings, had just decided to follow Him (new converts).

The burning desire in the heart of a disciple of the Lord Jesus Christ is to know His way. When Thomas asked Him to show them the way, He said:

> *I am the way, the truth, and the life: no man cometh unto the Father, but by me.* (John 14: 6)

The Lord Jesus (Yeshua) is **the Way** we are to follow, **the Truth** we are to believe and **the Life** we are to live.

A disciple is one who believes in the doctrines of a teacher or a school of thoughts and follows to learn. The word 'disciple' was rarely used in the Old Testament. In the book of Isaiah it is used to refer to those that follow the testimony of the Lord and His Law (Isaiah 8: 16). It was also used for those that followed John the Baptist, those that followed the Pharisees (Mark 2: 18), and in the claim of the Pharisees that they were disciples of Moses (John 9: 28). In the New Testament, the word disciple is used mainly for the followers of the Lord Jesus Christ.

The Lord has committed the gospel of the kingdom to His disciples to take to the whole world. Before He left to return to His Father in heaven, He commissioned them, saying:

> . . . *All power is given unto me in heaven and in earth. Go ye therefore, and teach all nations, baptizing them in the name of the Father, and of the Son, and of the Holy Ghost: Teaching them to observe all things whatsoever I have commanded you: and, lo, I am with you alway,* even *unto the end of the world. Amen.* (Matthew 28: 18-20)

Clearly, the message of the gospel is to be spread by making disciples. The work of the gospel of the kingdom is suffering today because many are busy making converts, instead of disciples. It is upon us to ponder our ways to see if we've been keeping to the command of the Lord. If we judge ourselves, we shall not be judged. The thing that is inevitable, is the fact that in the end, it shall be required of each of us to give account of all our works before the Lord (I Corinthians 3: 13).

The Lord has laid down the principles of the way of life we are to lead, if we are to walk in His footsteps to do the work of the kingdom of God. It is in the principles that His disciples are distinguished from the world, making them the light of the world and the salt of the earth.

CHAPTER 1

Discipleship

Discipleship in this context is the making of disciples of the doctrine of the kingdom of God. The disciples of the Lord Jesus (Yeshua) are those that believe His teachings and follow in His footsteps. Just before the Lord was received back into heaven, He gave a command to them to go and teach all nations to observe all things that He had taught them; which is what discipleship is all about.

> *And Jesus came and spake unto them, saying, All power is given unto me in heaven and in earth. Go ye therefore, and teach all nations, baptizing them in the name of the Father, and of the Son, and the Holy Ghost: Teaching them to observe all things whatsoever I have commanded you: and, lo, I am with you alway, even unto the end of the world. Amen.* (Matthew 28: 18-20)

It is clear from the above passage that we are to teach, that is, make Disciples of Christ's doctrine. If we are not careful we can be sidetracked into making converts. Should this happen, the result will be a following of people who only know the acts of the Lord, not His ways!

In the beginning of the Lord Jesus' ministry, He went about all Galilee, teaching in synagogues and preaching the gospel of the kingdom. As He ministered, He healed all manner of sicknesses and disease among the people and His fame went throughout all the regions around. As a result, a great multitude followed Him from Galilee, Decapolis, Jerusalem, Judea and from beyond Jordan (Matthew 4: 23-25).

The need for discipleship

As Jesus continued with His ministry to the people, the time came when He had to address the need to make disciples. In Mathew 5: 1-2, it is recorded that when the Lord saw the multitude, He went up a Mount and sat down. It is important to take note that this time He did not begin to preach the gospel of the kingdom, and heal the people as He usually did. He, instead, taught His disciples that went to Him; laying the foundation of the way of life they had to live if they were to come after Him.

We may wonder what was going on, because the multitude waited to be ministered to. Although the people were in desperate conditions, it was needful for the Lord to raise disciples. Therefore, instead of continuing with mass evangelism and healing of the people, He began the work of making disciples of His followers. In this, His ministry entered the phase of establishing His followers in His doctrine, so that they too could go out and do the same works He did.

Time comes, in every ministry, when the need to make disciples arises, but it is up to the leaders to recognise and address it. Such times are critical moments in ministry. If we miss them, the consequences will be dire. Leadership that ignore or fail to recognise the need to make disciples are bound to terminate their visions upon their respective departures. An effective leadership endeavours to train others to carry on with the work of the kingdom.

In order to spread a doctrine, the best way is to raise people who will be faithful to the teachings and teach others to do the same.

NEGLECT OF TEACHING

Neglect of teaching is the main reason for failure in making disciples today. The focus that is on mass evangelism has a lot to do with it. Many are concentrating their resources almost entirely on mass evangelism for mainly two reasons:

- Because of a lack of knowledge that by this method one can hardly make disciples.
- Because of love of fame.

Lack of knowledge

The focus of many servants of God is on mass evangelism, simply because they think this is the best way to reach the world with the gospel. However, the reality is that mass evangelism is the least effective method in spreading the message of the gospel. There is no better way of spreading the gospel than by making disciples.

Isn't it sad that many in the house of God have been led to believe that their work is to support those with big ministries? In light of the word of God, we see that leaders are, rather, to edify to perfection and prepare the saints for the work of the ministry (Ephesians 4: 11-13). The very people sitting in our pews are the ones we are to prepare to do the work of the ministry.

A pastor once did a simple survey during a service to stress this very point. He asked all the people who believed in the Lord Jesus during mass crusades to stand up, and shockingly, three people stood up out of a congregation of about 5,000 people. He then asked those that believed on the Lord during church meetings to stand up, and about 300 stood up. Finally he asked those that got born again because someone preached to them one on one, and the vast majority of the people in that assembly stood up!

Clearly, mass evangelism was proved, in this case, to be the least effective method in bringing people to believe in the Lord Jesus Christ.

If by mass evangelism we can hardly bring people into the kingdom, how on earth can we, by this method, be able to make disciples? It is mainly those that are taught one on one or in small groups that get to become established in the things of God. The early church grew strong because they met daily to be taught in the apostles' doctrine—in the temple, and in synagogues (in the case of those that were in Diaspora), as well as in smaller groups in homes.

Because we can hardly make disciples by mass evangelism, it is a mistake to focus entirely on it for doing the work of the kingdom.

We must be careful, though, not to go to the other extreme by rejecting it all together. Mass evangelism is important; Jesus did a lot of it. Where it is needful in the work of the kingdom is in the building of the people's faith in the power of God. This is particularly important to the unbelieving, because when they see the demonstration of the power of God in the miracles, signs, and wonders that accompany the gospel, their faith is built on the fact that the word of God has power (I Corinthians 2: 4-5).

Without addressing the need for discipleship, there is no ministry that can last.

If the Lord Jesus had not raised disciples to carry on with the work of the kingdom, His ministry would have ended when He returned to His Father in heaven. Clearly, the Lord's will for us is not to terminate the ministries He has given us, upon our departure. Rather, we are to leave them in the hands of others, who, in turn, are to teach others to carry on with them after they are gone.

Love of fame

Because mass evangelism is usually accompanied by miracles, signs and wonders, a lot of preachers tend to focus on it with the intent that they might become famous. Unless one's focus is on the vision, this can become a very difficult point in ministry. Any of us can easily be tempted to continue laying emphasis on the miraculous because they draw multitudes. The evidence that one has fallen into this temptation, is in the tendency to care more about numbers of attendance than the conditions of the souls of the people.

We learn from John the Baptist that a multitude of people who cannot bring fruit of repentance are heading straight to hell.

> *Then said he to the multitude that came forth to be baptized of him, O generation of vipers, who hath warned you to flee from the wrath to come? Bring forth therefore fruits worthy of repentance, and begin not to say within yourselves, We have Abraham to our father: for I say unto you, That God is able of these stones to raise up children unto Abraham. And now also the axe is laid unto the root of the trees: every*

tree therefore which bringeth not forth good fruit is hewn down, and cast into the fire. (Luke 3: 7-9)

A large following of people is not proof of the success of a ministry. John the Baptist did not take the multitude that went to him in the wilderness for a success, but dealt hard with them. He demanded that the people brought forth fruit worthy of repentance. In other words, he demanded that they depart from their evil ways.

It is an utter waste of time and irresponsible to lead a multitude of people who are not going to make it into heaven. We must be warned that the word of God charges with blood guiltiness ministers who do not declare the whole counsel of God!

Son of man, I have made thee a watchman unto the house of Israel: therefore hear the word at my mouth, and give them warning from me.

When I say unto the wicked, Thou shalt surely die; and thou givest him not warning, nor speakest to warn the wicked from his wicked way, to save his life; the same wicked man shall die in his iniquity; but his blood will I require at thine hand. (Ezekiel 3: 17-18)

If the people are not warned of the wrath to come, they'll perish, but notice, their blood will be required at the hands of those appointed to watch over them.

Yet if thou warn the wicked, and he turn not from his wickedness, nor from his wicked way, he shall die in his iniquity; but thou hast delivered thy soul.

Again, When a righteous man *doth turn from his righteousness, and commit iniquity, and I lay a stumblingblock before him, he shall die: because thou hast not given him warning, he shall die in his sin, and his righteousness which he hath* done *shall not be remembered; but his blood will I require at thine hand.*

Nevertheless if thou warn the righteous man, *that the righteous sin not, and he doth not sin, he shall surely live, because he is warned; also thou hast delivered thy soul.*
(Ezekiel 3: 19-21)

In declaring the whole counsel of God, we warn others, as well as deliver our own souls from blood guiltiness. Shall we, in the end, have clear consciences like Paul, for instance? At the end of his ministry to the Ephesians, he declared that he was free of the blood of all men because he had declared to them all the counsel of God (Acts 20: 26-27).

Knowing the terror of the Lord, we have to persuade men to turn from wickedness (II Corinthians 5: 11). Where fame of a ministry is more important than the salvation of souls, is not what you'd call church. A true soldier of Christ cannot compromise the massage of salvation for fame. It is better to have a small congregation of disciples than a multitude of people who are not.

JEALOUSY

There is a tendency to fear that others might become more anointed when they are made into disciples. This fear leads to jealousy. Ministers that fail to reject it are the most likely to keep the people they lead in ignorance of their full potential in Christ. If a disciple gets given grace to operate in more anointing, we have to praise God because there is no competition in the body of Christ. Each member operates according to the measure of grace given them where they are fitted in Christ.

A church, whose members are operating fully in the grace given them, is strong and healthy. Just as in the natural, a body whose members function effectively is healthy and strong.

It is important to always remember that the Spirit of God gives measures of grace differently to us, according to where we are fitted in the body. This, He does as He wills; we do not choose where and how to be used of the Lord. Those that fight others because of anointing that is revealed through them actually fight against the body of Christ.

We'll be saved from a lot of troubles if we reject jealousy and work to bring up all in the house of the Lord to function effectively where they have been placed in the body of Christ. It is a lot easier to lead a church whose members are full of the Spirit of God than one that is full of carnality. Regarding this, a good example to follow is that of Moses. He wished that all the people of God were filled with His Spirit (Numbers 11: 27-29).

HYPOCRISY

Many are failing to make disciples because they are busy teaching what they do not practice.

If our messages cannot effect change in our own lives, why should we expect them to bring change in other people's lives? Life and death are in the power of the tongue. That is why we must circumcise our lips so that we may bring word that can change people. If we speak in hypocrisy the Holy Ghost will be grieved with us. How then can we expect Him to trust us with the power of the very message we are disobeying?

For us to be effective in making disciples, it is a must that we practice what we teach. Paul said to Timothy, *The husbandman that laboureth must be first partaker of the fruits* (II Timothy 2: 6). The reason the early church was so effective in making disciples was because their lives were, in themselves, epistles to those they reached with the gospel. Paul for instance, time and again, told the churches he taught to follow him as he followed Christ (I Corinthians 11: I, 4: 16). How many of us can sincerely say this to the people we lead?

If our deeds are far from what we teach, what difference is there between us and what the Pharisees were? Their deeds were hypocritical because they did not practice what they taught (Matthew 23: 1-3). Hypocrisy is the leaven that the Lord Jesus has warned us to beware of.

> *In the mean time, when there were gathered together an innumerable multitude of people, insomuch that they trode one upon another, he began to say unto his disciples first of all, Beware ye of the leaven of the Pharisees, which is hypocrisy.* Luke 12: 1)

Pray our deeds become what we preach and teach, for it is a matter of life and death.

CHAPTER 2

The beatitudes

The beatitudes are spiritual well-being and prosperity that are rewarded for walking in the way of the Lord. They describe the disciples of the kingdom of heaven, and their rewards, both in the present and in the life to come.

The Lord began making His followers into disciples, by teaching them those values that would earn them blessings from His Father in heaven.

> *And he opened his mouth, and taught them, saying, Blessed* are *the poor in spirit: for their's is the kingdom of heaven. Blessed* are *they that mourn: for they shall be comforted. Blessed* are *the meek: for they shall inherit the earth. Blessed* are *they which do hunger and thirst after righteousness: for they shall be filled. Blessed* are *the merciful: for they shall obtain mercy.*

Blessed are *the pure in heart: for they shall see God. Blessed* are *the peacemakers: for they shall be called the children of God. Blessed* are *they which are persecuted for righteousness' sake: for their's is the kingdom of heaven. Blessed are ye, when* men *shall revile you, and persecute* you, *and shall say all manner of evil against you falsely, for my sake. Rejoice, and be exceeding glad: for great* is *your reward in heaven: for so persecuted they the prophets which were before you.* (Matthew 5: 2-12)

The Lord's disciples are set apart from the world, in character and lifestyle, by the way they are ordained to walk in. To the world the values that the Lord is teaching here are considered weaknesses of character, but in the kingdom of heaven they prepare God's people to receive strength and power from Him.

POVERTY IN SPRIT

The poor in spirit are blessed with inheritance of the kingdom of heaven. Poverty in spirit is spiritual bankruptcy or total dependency on God for everything. It is not until we empty ourselves of our own wisdom and knowledge that we can become like (or gain) Christ. He was totally dependent on God for everything, as is revealed in the following verses of scripture wherein He said:

"My Father worketh hitherto, and I work." (John 5: 17).

. . . Verily, verily, I say unto you, The Son can do nothing of himself, but what he seeth the Father do: for what things soever he doeth, these also doeth the Son likewise (John 5: 19).

I can of mine own self do nothing: as I hear I judge: and my judgement is just; because I seek not mine own will, but the will of the Father which hath sent me. (John 5: 30)

In acknowledging that it was His Father at work in everything He did, the Lord Jesus has clearly shown us what it means to be poor in spirit. Why we have to strip ourselves off of our own wisdom and understanding is because we cannot receive the things of God in carnality.

Now we have received, not the spirit of the world, but the spirit which is of God; that we might know the things that are freely given to us of God. Which things also we speak, not in the words which man's wisdom teacheth, but which the Holy Ghost teacheth; comparing spiritual things with spiritual. But the natural man receiveth not the things of the Spirit of God: for they are foolishness unto him: neither can he know them, *because they are spiritually discerned.* (I Corinthians 2: 12-14)

Those who are strong in themselves depend on their own wisdom and understanding, and, therefore, cannot seek or receive the kingdom of heaven.

It is not until we reach the point where we acknowledge that we can do nothing without God that we can be entrusted with His power.

Beware of presumption

One of the ways we can fail to maintain spiritual bankruptcy is if we are presumptuous. There is, in us, a tendency to depend on our experiences of the past instead of seeking to follow the leading of the Spirit of God. Where we fail to resist this temptation, our past successes become greater hindrances to us than the enemy. After which, ministry is by routine instead of drawing strength from the Spirit of God. The best thing to do with experiences of the past is to forget them. Paul said in his letter to the Philippians that he forgot the past so that he could press forward to reach the things that were before him.

> *Brethren, I count not myself to have apprehended: but* this *one thing* I do, *forgetting those things which are behind, and reaching forth unto those things which are before, I press toward the mark for the prize of the high calling of God in Christ Jesus.* (Philippians 3: 13-14)

If we are already decided to go about in ministry the same ways we have done in the past, then the Spirit of God is not in what we are doing. We must be warned that God hates routine. In fact, routine is a form of superstition, and superstition is a manifestation of the spirit of witchcraft.

We cannot predict God because His ways are not our ways—The only way to know how He will do things in the future is to seek the knowledge from Him.

> *For my thoughts* are *not your thoughts, neither* are *your ways my ways, saith the LORD. For* as *the heavens are higher than the earth, so are my ways higher than your ways, and my thoughts than your thoughts.* (Isaiah 55: 8-9)

Unless we maintain spiritual bankruptcy in our lives, we won't gain the knowledge of God.

MOURNING

The kind of mourning the Lord is teaching here is rewarded with a blessing of comfort. One of the ways we learn to know the Lord in the fellowship of His suffering, is in mourning, for He was a man of sorrows and acquainted with grief (Isaiah 53: 3). His grief was over the lost, in intercession to move God's hand to bring them salvation.

Mourning in intercession is not to be associated with the negative because it is a means by which we go deep into travail when seeking the face of the Lord. When pain is so great, there comes a time when one can only mourn and groan without uttering a word.

Intercession is deeply rooted in love

The work of intercession is deeply rooted in love. The cry of a supplicant is "mercy, Lord". Love is kind—If we abide in love, we abide in God because God is love. He is compassionate towards the afflicted, to deliver them regardless of the cause of their troubles. Some of the people that the Lord redeemed in Psalms 107, for example, were afflicted through faults of their own, and some of them by reasons beyond their control.

1. Some of them wandered in the wilderness, in a solitary way, finding no city to dwell in. Then they cried unto the Lord in their trouble, and He delivered them out of their distress (Psalms 107: 4-7).
2. Some were in darkness and in the shadow of death, being bound in affliction and iron because they rebelled against the words of God, and contemned His counsel. Then they cried unto the Lord in their trouble, and He delivered them out of their distress (Psalms 107: 10-13).
3. Some were afflicted because of their transgressions and iniquities to the point that they could not eat and were at

the point of death. Then they cried unto the Lord in their trouble, and He saved them out of their distresses. He sent His word, and healed them, and delivered them from their destructions (Psalms 107: 17-20).

4. Some were tossed about on the sea upon the high waves. They cried unto the Lord in their trouble, and He brought them out of their distress, calming the storm such that the waves were still (Psalms 107: 23-30).

The four groups of people described above were able to cry unto the Lord in their distresses. However, a lot of people cry because of their affliction, but do not know how to call on the name of the Lord to save them. Such people need someone who can stand in the gap for them, to seek the Lord to deliver them out of their troubles.

For instance, when Israel was in bondage in Egypt, they sighed and cried by reason of their bondage.

> *And it came to pass in process of time, that the king of Egypt died: and the children of Israel sighed by reason of the bondage, and they cried, and their cry came up unto God by reason of the bondage.* (Exodus 2: 23)

God, in His mercy, saw their affliction and chose Moses to lead them out of bondage. Also we learn in the book of James that the cries of the oppressed have reached the ears of the Lord of hosts (the Lord of the heavenly armies) (James 5: 1-6). He will bring financial judgement on the rich for defrauding the poor that reaped their fields.

> *Behold, the hire of the labourers who have reaped down your fields, which is of you kept back by fraud, crieth: and the cries of them which have reaped are entered into the ears of the Lord of sabaoth.* (James 5: 4)

God has chosen His people to be vessels through whom He brings salvation to many who would otherwise not cry to Him for help.

We cannot stand in the gap for individuals or nations, if we are not touched by their sufferings. The Lord Jesus is teaching us to be compassionate, that we may be concerned and pray to move God's hand into situations affecting people all around us. In so doing, we become like Him, for He is full of love. When He saw the multitudes that came after Him, faint and having no shepherd, He was moved to minister to them to rid them of their pain and sorrows.

> *But when he saw the multitudes, he was moved with compassion on them, because they fainted, and were scattered abroad, as sheep having no shepherd. Then saith he unto his disciples, The harvest truly is plenteous, but the labourers are few; Pray ye therefore the Lord of the harvest, that he will send forth labourers into his harvest.* (Matthew 9: 36-38)

God looks for a man to stand in the gap

When judgement is looming God looks for a man to intercede that He may save. He has no pleasure in the destruction of the wicked, but desires that they turn back to Him (Ezekiel 33: 11). However, those that are dead in their transgressions cannot hear the calling of the Lord unto repentance. This is where the ministry of intercession is important. The Lord looks for a man, from amongst His servants, to stand in the gap, to confess and repent the sins of the individuals or nations, so that they may be saved.

The mark of all true intercession

Selfless concern is the mark of all true intercession. This is a kind of prayer whereby we confess the sins of others like we ourselves are involved in it. Take for instance, Daniel—although he was a righteous man, in his intercessory prayer for the nation of Israel, he confessed the sins of the people like he himself was involved in it.

> *And I prayed unto the LORD my God, and made my confession, and said, O Lord, the great and dreadful God, keeping the covenant and mercy to them that love him, and to them that keep his commandments;*
>
> *We have sinned, and have committed iniquity, and have done wickedly, and have rebelled, even by departing*

from thy precepts and from thy judgments: Neither have we hearkened unto thy servants the prophets, which spake in thy name to our kings, our princes, and our fathers, and to all the people of the land. (Daniel 9: 4-7)

O Lord, to us belongeth *confusion of face, to our kings, to our princes, and to our fathers, because we have sinned against thee.*

To the Lord our God belong *mercies and forgivenesses, though we have rebelled against him; Neither have we obeyed the voice of the LORD our God, to walk in his laws, which he set before us by his servants the prophets. Yea, all Israel have transgressed thy law, even by departing, that they might not obey thy voice; therefore the curse is poured upon us, and the oath that is written in the law of Moses the servant of God, because we have sinned against him.* (Daniel 9: 8-11)

Burdens are conceived

Burdens of intercession are conceived like the child of a womb. They are carried for as long as is appointed of the Lord, and then travailed with to bring forth the intended results. This explains the attachment of intercessors to those whom they carry before the Lord. Just as a mother can quite readily take the position of her child in punishment, intercessors readily pray or which to be punished instead. For instance, Moses repented the sins of Israel to the point that he prayed to God to blot him out of His book, instead of destroying His people (Exodus 32: 31-32). Paul too wished to be accursed from Christ for Israel's sake (Romans 9: 1-4).

The greatest intercessor is the Lord Jesus. He came and took the sins of the world upon Himself (took our place) and bore the penalty.

> *. . . he hath poured out his soul unto death: and he was numbered with the transgressors; and he bare the sin of many, and made intercession for the transgressors.* (Isaiah 53: 12)

The Lord stood in the gap, even the great gulf that separated man from God and made intercession, pouring out His soul unto death.

God is not asking us to pay the penalty for the sins of the wicked. The Lord Jesus has already taken the sins of the world upon Himself and paid the penalty on the cross at Golgotha. What we are required to do is to intercede for the wicked, repenting their sins so that they may be saved.

Are we faithful to the call?

If God looks for a man to stand in the gap for a nation or individuals, but finds none, He, in His mercy, brings salvation for them by some other means—but we must be warned that those that could have interceded do not go unpunished. For instance, in the days of Isaiah, when the Lord looked for one to make intercession for Israel, but found none—His own arm brought her salvation.

> *And judgement is turned away backward, justice standeth afar off: for truth is fallen in the street, and equity cannot enter. Yea, truth faileth; and he that departeth from evil maketh himself a prey: and the Lord saw it, and it displeased him that there was no judgement. And he saw that there was no man, and wondered that there was no intercessor: therefore his arm brought salvation unto him; and his righteousness, it sustained him.* (Isaiah 59: 14-16)

The Lord wondered that there was no intercessor and, in compassion, rose up to bring Israel salvation. Why it is a wonder when there is no intercessor found from amongst God's people, is because they are supposed to be full of love and compassionate.

Considering what is going on in the world today, isn't it a wonder, if we go about unconcerned? We have to wake up to the fact that indifference is sin. The prophet Samuel said that he would not sin against the Lord in ceasing to pray for Israel.

> *Moreover as for me, God forbid that I should sin against the LORD in ceasing to pray for you: but I will teach you the good and the right way:* (I Samuel 12: 23)

To be in the position to intercede, and care not to do so, is sin against the Lord. He is displeased when those that He has saved by His grace do not care about others. We are all here today because the greatest intercessor, the Lord Jesus, stood in the gulf that separated us from God, and made intercession for us. Shouldn't we be concerned for others who are still dead in their transgressions, to bring them to the foot of the cross through intercession?

Shall we not learn from the warning that Mordecai gave Esther? He said that if she kept quiet, deliverance would rise for Israel by some other means, but as for her and her father's household, they would be destroyed (Esther 4: 13-14). Clearly, one that doesn't care to supplicate when he (or she) is supposed to doesn't go unpunished.

The indifferent are not spared

The unconcerned get punished with the wicked when God's judgement falls. For instance, those that did not care to be concerned about the sins in the city of Jerusalem perished with evil doers in the judgement thereof. Before the Lord judged the city, He sent His angel to set marks on those that mourned and wept because of all the sins that was in it.

And the Lord said unto him, Go through the midst of
the city, through the midst of Jerusalem, and set a mark

upon the foreheads of men that sigh and that cry for
all the abominations that be done in the midst thereof.
(Ezekiel 9: 4)

It was only those who mourned for the sins of Jerusalem that were spared from the judgement that fell on the city.

If there be indifference because of a mentality that the wicked deserve their punishment, it is a shame. True, they deserve them, but we must remember that we also were transgressors and deserved to be judged, but Christ took our place because of God's mercy on us.

Chances for intercession can be lost

The time God gives an individual or a nation to turn away from wickedness, does not go on forever. The only chances we have for intercession for individuals or nations are before their sins reach the full measure for judgement. After which, God will no longer hold His judgement, even if someone rises to intercede for them. For instance, God told Jeremiah that even if intercessions were made for Judah by Moses and Samuel, He would not listen. This was because the iniquity of Judah had reached the full measure for judgement in the sight of God.

Then said the LORD unto me, Though Moses and Samuel
stood before me, yet my mind could not be toward this

people: cast them *out of my sight, and let them go forth.*
(Jeremiah 15: 1)

In this, the Lord was telling Jeremiah not to intercede for Judah because her time of judgement had come. About that period of time, the elders of Israel that were in captivity gathered before Ezekiel to inquire if the land would be saved as their prophets were prophesying. One of the things that the Lord told Ezekiel to tell the elders was that even if Noah, Daniel and Job were in the land, their intercessions would not save the people, but only themselves.

> *Though these three men, Noah, Daniel, and Job, were in it, they should deliver* but *their own souls by their righteousness, saith the Lord GOD.* (Ezekiel 14: 14)

There was a lost opportunity to intercede for the nation of Israel before her iniquity was full. This is revealed in the twenty second chapter of the book of Ezekiel. The Lord sent word through Prophet Ezekiel, telling the children of captivity the reasons why judgement fell on them. It was because there was a long chronicle of failures of every group, without anyone caring to stand up for righteousness.

- There was a conspiracy of her prophets—they were like a roaring lion ravening the prey—they devoured souls—they took the treasure and precious things—they made many widows in their midst (murdered the husbands of many women).

- Her priests violated the Law—profaned God's holy things—they showed no difference between the clean and the unclean—they hid their eyes from the Lord's Sabbath (they did not keep the Sabbath)—they profaned the name of the Lord.

- Her princes were like wolves ravening the prey—they shed blood—destroyed souls—got dishonest gain.

When all this wickedness was taking place, the prophets, instead of confronting the evil, dubbed (covered up) everything with false messages. Clearly, they were unfaithful in bringing the oracles of God to the people. If they themselves were wicked, how could they take a stand against all the evil that was going on? Since the leadership was corrupt, the people of the land followed suit.

- They used oppression—exercised robbery—vexed the poor and needy—oppressed the stranger wrongfully.

When all this evil was going on, the Lord did not just wait for the sin of the land to be full and then bring judgement. He looked for a man to intercede for the land, but sadly, found none!

And I sought for a man among them, that should make up the hedge, and stand in the gap before me for the land, that I should not destroy it: but I found none. Therefore

have I poured out mine indignation upon them; I have consumed them with the fire of my wrath: their own way have I recompensed upon their heads, saith the Lord GOD.
(Ezekiel 22: 30-31)

The leadership was so corrupt that from amongst the priesthood and the prophets, there was none that had a heart to stand in the gap for Israel. The Lord would no longer hold His judgement. Therefore, He poured out His indignation upon the land. Had there been a man to intercede for her, she could have been saved.

Jeremiah mourned the lost opportunity to intercede for Israel, saying:

The harvest is past, the summer is ended, and we are not saved. For the hurt of the daughter of my people am I hurt; I am black; astonishment hath taken hold on me. Is there *no balm in Gilead;* is there *no physician there? why then is not the health of the daughter of my people recovered?*
(Jeremiah 8: 20-22)

Yes, there could have been balm in Gilead, had the opportunity to behold the face of the Lord on behalf of Israel not been lost. Her priests and prophets could have stood in the gap for her, but they had corrupted themselves (Ezekiel 22: 25-26).

Up to the time when judgement was looming, the leadership was still corrupted. Jeremiah was grieved because of the false ministry to the people, and lamented about it, saying:

> *For from the least of them even unto the greatest of them every one* is *given to covetousness; and from the prophet even unto the priest every one dealeth falsely. They have healed also the hurt* of the daughter *of my people slightly, saying, Peace, peace; when* there is *no peace.* (Jeremiah 6: 13-14)

The Lord spoke to Jeremiah of the leadership of Israel at that time, saying:

> *Were they ashamed when they had committed abomination? nay, they were not at all ashamed, neither could they blush: therefore they shall fall among them that fall: at the time* that *I visit them they shall be cast down, saith the LORD.* (Jeremiah 6: 15)

Moreover, the Lord spoke to Jeremiah concerning the leaders, telling him that He had pleaded with them to turn back to Him, but they would not listen to His voice. He had spoken to them, saying, Stand ye in the ways, and see, and ask for the old paths, wherein is the good way, and walk therein, and ye shall have rest for your souls. But, they answered Him, saying, "We will not walk therein". The Lord had also set watchmen over them, saying,

Hearken to the sound of the trumpet. But, they answered, saying, "We will not hearken" (Jeremiah 6: 16-17). Surely, this was a leadership that failed the nation.

We have to understand that the intercessions of Jeremiah and Ezekiel could not stop the carrying away of Judah into captivity. This was because her iniquity had reached the full measure for judgement during the days of King Manasseh. In fact, the iniquities of both kingdoms, Israel and Judah, had reached the full, way before the times of Jeremiah and Ezekiel. God had determined to carry Israel into captivity in the days of King Pekah son of Ramaliah (Isaiah 7: 8, II Kings 15: 29), and the kingdom of Judah, because of the sins of King Manasseh (II Kings 21: 11-15).

For the Lord's name's sake

Where we are to be concerned for the Lord's name's sake is amongst His people. In sinning, they profane His name. Should God's judgement fall on them, the heathen will not see that it is because of their sin, but question where their God is.

One of the reasons Moses stood in the gap for Israel was because he was concerned for the Lord's name's sake. He pleaded with the Lord that if He destroyed the children of Israel in the wilderness, the Egyptians would say that He brought them there for mischief, to consume them from the face of the earth.

And Moses besought the LORD his God, and said, LORD,
why doth thy wrath wax hot against thy people, which
thou hast brought forth out of the land of Egypt with great
power, and with a mighty hand? Wherefore should the
Egyptians speak, and say, For mischief did he bring them
out, to slay them in the mountains, and to consume them
from the face of the earth?

Turn from thy fierce wrath, and repent of this evil
against thy people. Remember Abraham, Isaac, and Israel,
thy servants, to whom thou swarest by thine own self, and
saidst unto them, I will multiply your seed as the stars
of heaven, and all this land that I have spoken of will
I give unto your seed, and they shall inherit it for ever.
(Exodus 32: 11-13)

Again Moses was concerned for the Lord's name's sake when He
wanted to destroy the children of Israel when they believed the
evil reports of ten of the spies and refused to enter the Promised
Land. He (Moses) interceded, saying that the heathen would
take it that the Lord was not able to bring Israel to the land He
promised them (Numbers 14: 15-16).

And Moses said unto the LORD, Then the Egyptians shall
hear it, (for thou broughtest up this people in thy might
from among them;) And they will tell it to the inhabitants
of this land: for they have heard that thou LORD art
among this people, that thou LORD art seen face to face,

and that *thy cloud standeth over them, and* that *thou goest before them, by day time in a pillar of a cloud, and in a pillar of fire by night. Now* if *thou shalt kill* all *this people as one man, then the nations which have heard the fame of thee will speak, saying, Because the LORD was not able to bring this people into the land which he sware unto them, therefore he hath slain them in the wilderness.* (Numbers 14: 13-16)

Is there not a cause to be concerned for the Lord's name's sake, seeing the condition of His house today? How long are we going to wait before we shed tears because of all that is bringing shame in His house? When the glory of the Lord is missing from amongst His people, it is not something to be taken lightly.

The fearful thing about this is in the picture given us in the book of Joel in chapter two. If there is no fire on our altars, there is no point standing before it to offer sacrifices to God. The best thing to do in such situations is for the leaders to call solemn assemblies and together with the congregations, weep between the pouches and the altars. The Lord Himself gives us the prayer points for this gathering:

Let the priests, the ministers of the LORD, weep between the porch and the altar, and let them say, Spare thy people, O LORD, and give not thine heritage to reproach, that the heathen should rule over them: wherefore should they say among the people, Where is their God? (Joel 2: 17)

This is a prayer of repentance, weeping that our sins and those of the entire household of God be forgiven, so that we may not be given to reproach. Otherwise, the heathen will ask where our God is. Paul said that we ought to pray always in the Spirit, with all prayer and supplication, for all saints.

Praying always with all prayer and supplication in the Spirit, and watching thereunto with all perseverance and supplication for all saints; (Ephesians 6: 18)

We are a family. The conditions of others in the body should concern us, for our Father's name's sake and because of brotherly love.

This hour needs wet-eyed intercessors

From the conditions of the nations we see that we are in desperate need of spiritual awakening. Therefore, it is going to take praying with much weeping, mourning, fasting and travail to touch this generation. In such times we are to be afflicted in our souls, and weep: our laughter is to be turned into mourning and our joy into heaviness (James 4: 9).

These days, there seems to be far too much focus on rejoicing. Rejoicing is good, because the joy of the Lord is our strength. However, there is a season, and a time to every purpose under heaven (Ecclesiastes 3: 1). When we need revival, rejoicing does not help. Revival comes through prayers with weeping, mourning, fasting, and travail. This needs a level of intercession that takes hold of us and consumes us, to the point that we bear the burdens before the Lord continually.

The joy that awaits us at the harvest, no words can adequately express, for God has promised that those that sow in tears shall come rejoicing, bringing in their sheaves.

> *They that sow in tears shall reap in joy. He that goeth forth and weepeth, bearing precious seed, shall doubtless come again with rejoicing, bringing his sheaves* with him. (Psalms 126: 5-6)

Imagine the Lord Himself comforting us after we have mourned that His purposes be established on the earth, what word can describe that?

In conclusion, we are duty bound to make prayer and supplications for all men. Paul in his second epistle to Timothy urged that prayer and supplication be made for all men and for those in authority.

I exhort therefore, that, first of all, supplications, prayers, intercessions, and *giving of thanks, be made for all men; For kings, and* for *all that are in authority; that we may lead a quiet and peaceable life in all godliness and honesty.* (I Timothy 2: 1-2)

We have been called out of the kingdom of darkness into God's marvellous light that we may show forth, in this world, the praise of Him that saved us. Creation is groaning, awaiting the manifestations of the sons of God. Shall we not groan and mourn, making supplications that the will of God be done on the earth as it is in heaven?

MEEKNESS

The meek are those that won't fight back. The Lord teaches that such people shall inherit the earth. He perfectly demonstrated what it means to be meek when the soldiers of the chief priests and the elders came to arrest Him in the Garden of Gethsemane. When Peter cut off the ear of a servant of the high priest in an attempt to defend Him, He rebuked him, saying:

. . . Put up again thy sword into his place: for all they that take the sword shall perish with the sword. Thinkest thou that I cannot now pray to my Father, and he shall presently give me more than twelve legions of angels? But

how then shall the scriptures be fulfilled, that thus it must be? (Matthew 26: 52-54)

The Lord Jesus could have, if He chose to, prayed to God and immediately He would have been given more than twelve legions of angels to fight for Him. We are glad that He accepted the cross, for in His death He has reconciled man to God. He came to earth wearing an ornament of meekness, and was lowly so that the scripture might be fulfilled. From this, we learn that meekness is required of us so that we may fulfill the will of the Father for our lives.

It is only in meekness that we are able to receive the things of the kingdom of heaven.

At that time Jesus answered and said, I thank thee, O Father, Lord of heaven and earth, because thou hast hid these things from the wise and prudent, and hast revealed them unto babes. (Matthew 11: 25)

Lack of meekness is the most probable reason why some people that read the word and even memorise scriptures are not noticeably changed. Understanding of scripture is by the illumination of the word to our hearts by the Holy Ghost. The engrafted word that is able to save our souls can be received only in meekness (James 1: 21). Why we have to receive the word in meekness is because, the things that are rooted in our minds exalt themselves against the knowledge of God (II Corinthians 10: 4-5).

It is important for us to always remember that God resists the proud, but gives grace to the humble (I Peter 5: 5).

Any knowledge that is contrary to the word of God hinders us from receiving from the Lord. Unless we humble ourselves and count them as dung (rubbish), we won't be willing to cast them away that we may receive the word of God in their place.

The meek shall be rewarded with the inheritance of the earth because they are joint heirs with Christ, who owns everything.

HUNGER AND THIRST FOR RIGHTEOUSNESS

We are to hunger and thirst for righteousness so that we may be filled with the word of God and His Spirit. Each of us is responsible to create this hunger and thirst in our own hearts. If we are not desirous of the knowledge of God, we won't seek Him. The following are some of the things that show there is a lack of hunger and thirst for righteousness in one's life.

1. When one's Bible(s) gather dust on the shelves.
2. Not tarrying long in reading of the word and prayer. If we want to be filled with the knowledge of God, we are going to have to take quality time in His presence.

3. Lack of zeal for the work of the ministry.

Hardness of heart is the main reason why many do not hunger and thirst after righteousness. The things that harden the heart are un-confessed sins in the life of an individual. Proverbs 28: 13 teaches that he that covers his sins shall not prosper, but whosoever confesses and forsakes his sins shall have mercy.

The problem is, imbedded in us is a nature that always tries to cover our sins instead of confessing and repenting them. We inherited this nature from Adam. He got it at the fall in the Garden of Eden.

When the LORD God asked him, saying, *Where art thou?* (Genesis 3: 9), it was not because He did not know Adam's physical location, for who can hide from He who is everywhere? Neither was it because God did not know the spiritual state Adam and Eve were in. He knows our thoughts even before we think them, so how can we hide our spiritual state from Him? By asking Adam where he was, the Lord wanted him to confess, with his own lips, the spiritual state he was in so that he could be convicted and repent of his ways and be saved, but sadly, he didn't.

Unless we acknowledge our transgressions, we cannot be convicted—if we are not contrite we cannot repent—without repentance we cannot be saved.

Adam, instead of acknowledging his sin, tried to cover it up, blaming the woman and indirectly God because He gave him the woman (Genesis 3: 12). Also it is revealed in the book of Job that Adam hid his transgressions. In Job's defence against the accusations of his friends, he listed the things which he knew that if he did; he would deserve to be punished. One of them was, if he had covered his sins.

> *If I covered my transgressions as Adam, by hiding mine iniquity in my bosom:* (Job 31: 33)

Adam hardened his heart by trying to explain why he ate of the forbidden fruit, instead of acknowledging he had sinned.

Had he (Adam) confessed and repented his sins, our case could be different. We probably wouldn't have to contend with hardness of heart. Now all of us have to seek to be made free from this corruption, so that we may get contrite and broken before God. The way of intimacy with God is in brokenness. Unless we learn to take responsibility for our actions and repent, we won't be delivered from hardness of heart.

From the live of David, king of Israel, we see an example of a broken spirit and contrite heart. On the other hand, in King Saul we see an example of a hardened heart.

Hardened heart

King Saul was a kind of person who would not acknowledge his sins. Each time he was confronted by Samuel, he explained his actions instead of repenting them. He disobeyed the instruction to wait at Gilgal for seven days for Samuel to come to him to offer a sacrifice before the battle with the Philistines.

When the children of Israel saw that they were faced with a very big army of the Philistines, numerous in number as the sand that is upon the sea shore, they were distressed and hid themselves in caves, thickets, rocks, high places and pits. King Saul waited seven days and Samuel had not come yet. When he saw that the people scattered from him, he offered the sacrifice. As soon as he finished, Samuel came and Saul went to meet him to salute him.

Asked by Samuel what he had done, Saul, instead of acknowledging he had sinned in not obeying the instruction of the Lord, explained his actions. He gave Samuel his reasons for not waiting for him for the sacrifice:

> . . . *Because I saw that the people were scattered from me, and that thou camest not within the days appointed, and that the Philistines gathered themselves together at Michmash; Therefore said I, The Philistines will come down now upon me to Gilgal, and I have not made*

supplication unto the LORD: I forced myself therefore, and offered a burnt offering. (I Samuel 13: 11-12)

How many of us are inclined to explaining our actions instead of taking responsibility for them and repenting? We are living in the days when attempt is constantly being made to explain sin away. However, the fact is, sin cannot be explained away. Its remedy is only in remission by the atoning work of the blood of the Lamb.

When Saul disobeyed the command of the Lord in not destroying all the Amalekites with all their animals, he, again explained his actions instead of repenting. He had kept Agag, king of the Amalekites, alive. He also had kept alive the best of the sheep and of the oxen, fatlings, lambs and all that was good. When Samuel came to him at Gilgal, after he had returned there from battle with the Amalekites, he greeted Samuel, blessing the Lord for the victory. But, Samuel asked him, saying:

. . . *What* meaneth *then this bleating of the sheep in mine ears, and the lowing of the oxen which I hear?* (I Samuel 15: 14)

Instead of admitting he had transgressed the command of the Lord, Saul explained why he allowed the people to keep the best of the animals. In defence of his actions, he said:

> *. . . They have brought them from the Amalekites: for the people spared the best of the sheep and of the oxen, to sacrifice unto the LORD thy God; and the rest we have utterly destroyed.* (I Samuel 15: 15)

Samuel went on to confront Saul, showing him that he had not obeyed the voice of the Lord and had done evil. At that point, Saul argued with Samuel, claiming he had obeyed the voice of the Lord. Listen to what he said:

> *. . . Yea, I have obeyed the voice of the LORD, and have gone the way which the LORD sent me, and have brought Agag the king of Amalek, and have utterly destroyed the Amalekites. But the people took of the spoil, sheep and oxen, the chief of the things which should have been utterly destroyed, to sacrifice unto the LORD thy God in Gilgal.* (I Samuel 15: 20-21)

Samuel then said to Saul:

> *. . . Hath the LORD* as great *delight in burnt offerings and sacrifices, as in obeying the voice of the LORD? Behold, to obey* is *better than sacrifice,* and *to hearken than the fat of rams. For rebellion* is as *the sin of witchcraft, and stubbornness* is as *iniquity and idolatry. Because thou hast rejected the word of the LORD, he hath also rejected thee from* being *king.* (I Samuel 15: 22-23)

It was at that point that Saul admitted he had sinned, but take note of the fact that he did this after he had exhausted every means to explain his actions, in his attempt to plead not guilty!

This is the kind of spirit that is hardening the hearts of the vast majority of people today. Sin is not a mistake as many suppose these days, but is the transgression of the Law (I John 3: 4). A mistake can be excused, but the remedy of sin is only in remission by the atoning work of the blood of the Lamb. Therefore, we have to fight to change in ourselves that we may reject the tendency to explain ourselves when we sin. God is faithful and just to forgive us, and cleanse us from all unrighteousness, if we confess our sins (I John 1: 9).

A broken and contrite spirit

To be broken and contrite means to be crushed under conviction of one's transgressions, being full of remorse. It is brokenness and contrition of spirit that paves the way for us to reach intimacy with God. In Isaiah 57: 15, the Lord says:

> *For thus saith the high and lofty One that inhabiteth eternity, whose name is Holy; I dwell in the high and holy place, with him also that is of a contrite and humble spirit, to revive the spirit of the humble, and to revive the heart of the contrite ones.*

From the life of King David we see an example of someone with a broken and contrite spirit. David was always quick to admit his sins and repent. Whenever David sinned, his conscience bothered him. We see this in the following examples:

1. Psalms chapter 38 records one of the times when David's conscience bothered him after he had sinned. He sang in verses 3-8, and 17-18:

    There is *no soundness in my flesh because of thine anger; neither* is there any *rest in my bones because of my sin. For mine iniquities are gone over mine head: as an heavy burden they are too heavy for me. My wounds stink* and *are corrupt because of my foolishness. I am troubled; I am bowed down greatly; I go mourning all the day long. For my loins are filled with a loathsome* disease: *and* there is *no soundness in my flesh. I am feeble and sore broken: I have roared by reason of the disquietness of my heart.* (Psalms 38: 3-8)

    For I am *ready to halt, and my sorrow* is *continually before me. For I will declare mine iniquity; I will be sorry for my sin.* (Psalms 38: 17-18)

    If our consciences do not bother us when we sin, it is a strong indication that we have hardened hearts, the consciences having been seared with a hot iron.

2. When the Lord sent Prophet Nathan to confront David because of his adulterous relationship with Bathsheba, and the murder of her husband, he immediately admitted his sin, saying, *I have sinned against the LORD.* And Nathan said to David, *The Lord also hath put away thy sin; thou shalt not die.* (II Samuel 12: 1-14)

3. When David counted the children of Israel, his heart smote him and he said unto God,

> *. . . I have sinned greatly, because I have done this thing: but now, I beseech thee, do away the iniquity of thy servant; for I have done very foolishly.* (I Chronicles 21: 8)

David had no peace after he had counted the people because he had a broken spirit. Those that are strong in themselves take long and much convincing to be convicted of their sins. One, who goes about normally after sinning, as if nothing is wrong, has hardened heart. It is up to each of us to judge ourselves in this and cry to God to help us to get broken in spirit.

True repentance

There can be no true repentance without acknowledging our transgressions to the point that they weigh on us in godly sorrow. It is then, and only then, can we be brought to the realization that we deserve God's just judgment. It is godly sorrow that leads to repentance.

MARGARET WHITE

If we are not careful to reject doctrines that condemn contrition, we'll never be saved.

Many are today taking the scripture in Nehemiah 8: 10, which says: ". . . *for the joy of the LORD your strength*" out of context, and thus harden their hearts against repentance. People who get crushed under conviction because of their sins are told to rise up and rejoice, before they reach the point of repentance! We must understand that we reach the place of the altar only in repentance.

True, it is the joy of the Lord that is our strength, but let us be careful to find out how that can be. God gives strength to the weak.

> *He giveth power to the faint; and to* them that have *no might he increaseth strength.* (Isaiah 40: 29)

Someone who is not broken and contrite is not weak. Such people may sing "*the joy of the Lord is my strength*" as much as they like, but will not receive strength from the Lord.

The children of Israel who were told by the Levites and the priests to rejoice because the joy of the Lord was their strength had broken before the Lord in contrition (Nehemiah 8: 9-11). When Ezra read from the book of the Law of Moses, and the Levites caused the people to understand the reading, they realized that they had not walked according to the commandments of the

46

Lord. The result was, they were crushed in contrition and wept and wept in repentance.

We have to be careful to take note that Ezra and the Levites told the people to stop weeping and rejoice before the Lord, **after they had reached the point of brokenness and contrition**. There is no point in telling unrepentant people to rejoice because the joy of the Lord is their strength. Singing or reciting the scripture won't get them to receive strength from the Lord, however much they try.

God loves brokenness and contrition in us because He knows that in ourselves we cannot be right. Each time we sin, the way out for us is in repentance, for this is the point at which we receive the mercy of the Lord and His salvation.

The beauty of brokenness

It is through brokenness and contrition that we find such sweet relief that words cannot adequately describe. King David described the blessedness of one whose sins have been remitted in the following few words:

> *Blessed* is he whose *transgression* is *forgiven,* whose sin *is covered. Blessed* is *the man unto whom the LORD imputeth not iniquity, and in whose spirit* there is *no guile.* (Psalms 32: 1-2)

47

The transgressor finds true joy when his (or her) sins have been forgiven. David longed for this moment, when he was confessing his sin, saying; *Restore unto me the joy of thy salvation . . .* (Psalms 51: 12).

It is in the beauty of brokenness that intercessors find joy that no words can describe. Because they repent their sins and those of others in brokenness, they enjoy sweet, sweet time in the presence of the Lord. No intercessor wants to exchange such moments for anything.

In conclusion, the voice of the Lord is calling to us today, saying, Where are you? Where do you stand morally and spiritually? To what place are you directing your efforts? What are our answers to these questions? If we are sincere, we'll find that most of our efforts are going on covering our sins, instead of acknowledging and repenting them. For the sake of our eternal souls, it is urgent that we overcome this nature, for, *He that covereth his sins shall not prosper: but whoso confesseth and forsaketh* them *shall have mercy.* (Proverbs 28: 13)

MERCY

The Lord is merciful to the merciful, but to the unmerciful He shows no mercy.

> *For he shall have judgment without mercy, that hath shewed no mercy; and mercy rejoiceth against judgment.* (James 2: 13)

In Psalms 18: 25-26, the Lord says:

> *With the merciful thou wilt shew thyself merciful; with an upright man thou wilt shew thyself upright; With the pure thou wilt shew thyself pure; and with the forward thou wilt shew thyself forward.*

It is expected of us to be merciful to others, firstly because we ourselves aren't without fault and, therefore, in need mercy. We are forgiven our sins as we forgive others their trespasses against us. Clearly, this means that if we are merciless, we won't make it into life. Secondly, we are to be merciful because God our Father is merciful. When we show mercy on others we become like Him.

HOLINESS

Holiness is required of us because God is holy. Only the pure in heart shall be given the blessing of seeing Him. Following after holiness is, therefore, a must (Hebrews 12: 14)—beginning right away as we come to the Lord, because the way that leads to life is the way of holiness. The unclean cannot walk in it, but the redeemed.

> *And an highway shall be there, and a way, and it shall be called the way of holiness; the unclean shall not pass over it; . . .* (Isaiah 35: 8)

The fact that the Lord has commanded us to be holy means we can attain holiness. We are destined to be a glorious church without any spot or wrinkle (Ephesians 5: 27). Holiness is maintained in us by the washing of the water of the word (Ephesians 5: 26), and by continually washing our robes in the blood of the Lamb (Revelations 7: 14). The Lord Jesus prayed to the Father that we may be sanctified by truth; His word (John 17: 17). It is, therefore, our duty to receive the word of truth that we may be holy.

What separates us from God is compromise of holiness in our lives.

> Behold, the LORD'S hand is not shortened, that it cannot save; neither his ear heavy, that it cannot hear: But your iniquities have separated between you and your God, and your sins have hid his face from you, that he will not hear.
> (Isaiah 59: 1-2)

Yet, sadly, today morals are in decline even right in the house of God! Indecency, impure language, idolatry and things sacrificed to idols are what are defiling God's people.

Where is holiness? How many preach and practice it? The few that are trying to do something about it have become legalistic, dealing hard only with women's dressing. Their failure in recognising other things that defile, that they have brought right in their midst, is a degree of blindness that is so profound. Holiness is not only about dressing, but is also about the sort of atmosphere we create in our midst and the thoughts of our minds.

Our thoughts are affected by the things we take in through our five senses. Philippians 4: 8 teaches us to overcome evil thoughts by thinking on whatsoever things are true, honest, just, pure, lovely, of good report; things of virtue and praise.

The battle to renew our minds is fierce, because these are the days when impurity is readily available in reading, audio and viewing materials. King David said he would walk within his house with a perfect heart and set no wicked thing before his eyes (Psalms 101: 2-3). We have been commanded not to touch the unclean thing that we may be received by the Lord (II Corinthians 6: 17). Those that wear clothing or things with images of the serpent, monsters, demonic ensigns such as skull and bones and such like, are playing with fire.

What we do in secret matters—we must be holy in them just as we are in the things that we do before men.

Christ loves the Church and gave Himself for her that He might sanctify and cleanse her with the washing of the water of the word, that He might present her to Himself a glorious Church, not having spot, or wrinkle, or any such thing; that she should be holy and without blemish (Ephesians 5: 25-27).

If we are not reading and meditating on the word of God as we ought to, how can we be holy? There is no short cut—Christian radio and television are good, but they will never replace the requirement for personal meditation on God's word. We are going to have to fill ourselves with the word of God and meditate in it day and night in order for us to do according to all that is written (Joshua 1: 8).

MAKING PEACE

Peacemakers are blessed because they shall be called the children of God. The greatest peacemaker is the Messiah, the only begotten Son of God. He came to earth to reconcile man with God in His atoning death on the cross at Golgotha. He has made peace between the Father and those that believe in Him by sowing fruit of righteousness in them. We are called to make peace amongst our fellow men because God's righteousness now resides in us by the Lord Jesus Christ, through whom true peace has come into the world.

> *And the fruit of righteousness is sown in peace of them that make peace.* (James 3: 18)

Those that make peace sow the fruit of righteousness amongst feuding parties. They are conformed to the likeness of the Lord Jesus, and therefore, are children of God.

SUFFERING FOR RIGHTEOUSNESS' SAKE

Persecution is part of the package of the things we receive in this life for following the Lord (Mark 10: 29-30). In Christ's last address to His disciples before His death, one of the things He told them was:

> *Remember the word that I said unto you, The servant is not greater than his lord. If they have persecuted me, they will persecute you; it they have kept my saying, they will keep yours also. But all these things will they do unto you for my name's sake, because they know not him that sent me.* (John 15: 20-21)

The way we are walking is narrow, and hedged with trials and temptations. There are also floods and fire to go through along the way.

> *When thou passest through the waters, I will be with thee; and through the rivers, they shall not overflow thee: when thou walkest through the fire, thou shalt not be burned; nether shall the flame kindle upon thee.* (Isaiah 43: 2)

Because it is when, not if, it means it is only a matter of time—we'll go through the waters and the fire. If our faith can hold to the end, we shall be saved. We see also in Paul's letter to the Corinthians that we suffer for righteousness sake so that the ministry is not blamed.

> *Giving no offence in any thing, that the ministry be not blamed: But in all things approving ourselves as the ministers of God, in much patience, in afflictions, in necessities, in distresses, In stripes, in imprisonments, in tumults, in labours, in watchings, in fastings;* (II Corinthians 6: 3-5)

The Lord allows tribulations in our lives to benefit us in shaping us for His purpose.

- God' strength is revealed in weakness.

Paul wrote, explaining to the Corinthian church how he leant that God's strength is revealed in weakness.

> *And he said unto me, My grace is sufficient for thee: for my strength is made perfect in weakness. Most gladly therefore will I rather glory in my infirmities, that the power of Christ may rest on me. Therefore I take pleasure in infirmities, in reproaches, in necessities, in persecutions, in distresses for Christ's sake: for when I am weak, then am I strong.* (II Corinthians 12: 9-10)

Paul treasured the things that he suffered, because they weakened his flesh and as a result, the power of God was revealed in him. Equally important is the fact that his weaknesses kept him so humble that he recognised that he had no reason to boast.

God allows us to go through things that weaken so that the power of Christ may rest upon us. He chose to put the treasure of the kingdom of heaven in us, vessels of weakness (earthen vessels), that the excellence of the power may be of God, not of us (II Corinthians 4: 7).

- We partake of Christ's suffering in the things we suffer.

By the things we suffer for righteousness sake we partake of the suffering of Christ, being made conformable unto His death. Unless we know Christ in the power of His resurrection, and in the fellowship of His sufferings, and are made conformable unto His death, we cannot have ultimate victory over our own flesh, the world and the devil. Paul cried out in his letter to the Philippians, revealing his longing to know Christ in this way, so that he would attain to the resurrection of the dead (Philippians 3: 10-11).

If we suffer with Christ, we shall be glorified with Him, and the glory that shall be revealed in us will make all our sufferings fade into nothing. In Romans 8: 18-19, Paul said:

> *For I reckon that the suffering of this present time are*
> *not worthy to be compared with the glory which shall*
> *be revealed in us. For the earnest expectation of the*
> *creature waiteth for the manifestation of the sons of God.*
> (Romans 8: 18-19)

When the sons of God shall be manifested (totally liberated from corruption), creation shall be set free from the bondage in which it was subjected at the fall. If it is through tribulations that we bear fruit by which we are liberated from the bondage, not only us, but creation also, then it is worth it all.

- We learn obedience by the things we suffer.

We learn from the book of Hebrews that the Lord Jesus learned obedience, and was perfected by the things which He suffered.

> *Though he were a Son, yet learned he obedience by the*
> *things which he suffered; And being made perfect, he*
> *became the author of eternal salvation unto all them that*
> *obey him;* (Hebrews 5: 8-9)

If it took our Lord and Master suffering to learn obedience, it will also take suffering for us to learn the same and be perfected. The things we suffer work in us to teach us obedience, and purity, bringing us into perfection like gold that is tried by fire. Job understood this very well, for he said:

But he knoweth the way that I take: when he hath tried me, I shall come forth as gold (Job 23: 10).

Due to the fact that tribulations (troubles) present us with the perfect conditions for learning to bear the fruit of the Spirit, we must thank God for them and bless those that trouble us. Because we've been given peace that surpasses all understanding, this is possible.

God gives sufficient grace

The Lord has not left us to go through the things we suffer helplessly, but through them all, He gives us grace and the power to overcome:

> *By pureness, by knowledge, by longsuffering, by kindness, by the Holy Ghost, by love unfeigned, By the word of truth, by the power of God, by the armour of righteousness on the right hand and on the left,* (II Corinthians 6: 6-7)

The Lord makes all things, whether negative or positive, to work out for our good.

> *By honour and dishonour, by evil report and good report: as deceivers, and* yet *true; As unknown, and* yet *well known; as dying, and behold we live; as chastened, and not killed; As sorrowful, yet always rejoicing; as poor yet*

making many rich; as having nothing, and yet *possessing all things.* (II Corinthians 6: 8-10)

We suffer by honour—It is almost hard to believe, but honour from men is a worse attack on us than dishonour. It all begins with receiving reward and salutations that members of the congregation and others give in appreciation for ministry. This sounds harmless and pleasant, but it is a very subtle and deadly poison. From this, the congregations gradually proceed to placing ministers on a pedestal!

We must beware that in receipt of honour from men is death of visions, for God will drop anyone that accepts to be lifted above His congregation. Therefore, we, being servants of the Lord, must never expect to be honoured for the works we do. Rather, each time we have served, we are to say that we are unprofitable servants because we only do what are our duties (Luke 17: 7-10).

By dishonour—It does not matter if we are dishonoured for the sake of the name of the Lord, because our reward is great in heaven.

As deceivers and yet true—when accused of deceit, for proclaiming the word of God, we rejoice because this is inevitable. The preaching of the cross is offensive to the unbelieving, yet it is the truth that can make the sinner free from sin.

As unknown, and yet well known—we are not known in this world, but are well known in heaven.

As dying, and behold we live; as chastened, and not killed—the psalmist said, "*Yea, for thy sake are we killed all day long; we are counted as sheep for the slaughter*" (Psalms 44: 22). Yet we live, because we have eternal life on the inside of us. We are battle-scarred, but destined to win. Paul said he bore in his body the marks of the Lord Jesus (Galatians 6: 17).

As sorrowful, yet always rejoicing—Our sorrows are over burdens given us by the Lord for the work of His kingdom. He takes our heavy burdens and gives us His yokes which are light. We rejoice because it is so fulfilling to be grieved that the work of the kingdom be done.

As poor, yet making many rich—We suffer loss of everything in this world to carry the gospel, but those that receive the Lord Jesus Christ are made rich in Him.

Beware of self-pity

As we run the race, we have to guard against self-pity, for it a giant that can bring us down. Job, for instance, was brought down by this giant to the level where he defended himself. He had endured brilliantly the loss of everything he had—his children, livestock, servants, and house (Job 1: 14-18). Instead of complaining and questioning why all this happened to him, Job rent his clothes, shaved his head and fell down and worshiped God, saying,

> . . . *Naked came I out of my mother's womb, and naked shall I return thither: the LORD gave, and the LORD hath taken away; blessed be the name of the LORD.* (Job 1: 21)

In Verse 22, the word of God testifies of Job, saying, "*In all this Job sinned not, nor charged God foolishly.*" Job passed the test with flying colours! How many of us question, and murmur against God when we suffer loss of a few things, let alone loosing everything.

After that, the devil obtained permission to touch Job's body, and he smote him with sore boils from the sole of his foot to his head. Job took a broken piece of pottery and used it to scrap himself. Something very dangerous happened at this point. The closest person to him, his wife, told him to curse God, and die (Job 1: 9). Job answered his wife, saying,

> . . . *Thou speakest as one of the foolish women speaketh. What? Shall we receive good at the hand of God, and shall we not receive evil? . . .* (Job 2: 10)

The above verse continues to say, "*In all this did not Job sin with his lips.*" Even when he was afflicted in his body, he did not open his mouth to question God, or complain against Him. Again, Job passed the test with flying colours! However, what happened next brought Job down to the level where he opened his mouth and said many things. As soon as he let self-pity to set in, he crumbled. What cause him to fall into self-pity were the lamentations of his three friends, E-li-phaz the te-man-ite, Bildad the Shuhite, and Zo-phar the Na-am-a-thite, who, on seeing Job's suffering, dramatised their grief.

When they looked from afar off and could not recognise him (Job), they lifted up their voices and wept, rending their clothes and sprinkling dust on their heads towards heaven! This kind of reaction is enough to finish off the afflicted person. We have to learn that sympathy, particularly if dramatised, doesn't help the afflicted. The right thing to do is to assure them of God's love and faithfulness.

As if their lamentations were not enough, the three friends of Job then sat down speechless for seven days, compounding the problem! At this, Job reached the breaking point. For the first time he opened his mouth and cursed the day he was born, saying:

> *Let the day perish wherein I was born, and the night* in which *it was said, There is a man child conceived. Let that day be darkness; let not God regard it from above, neither let the light shine upon it . . . Why died I not from the woumb?* why *did I* not *give up the ghost when I came*

*out of the belly? Why did the knees prevented me? Or why
the breasts that I should suck . . .* (Job 3: 3-26)

From the moment Job cursed the day he was born; his three friends switched sides to accuse him of being the cause of his problems due to sin in his life! What does that say about their dramatic lamentations? Were they really genuine? Job did extremely well until they appeared on the scene. He got into trouble because of the many words he spoke in defence against their (his friends') accusations.

The scripture teaches us in Proverbs 10: 19 that in a multitude of words there lacks not sin: but he that refrain his lips is wise.

After Job was done speaking in defence of himself, he was confronted for his much talking by his fourth friend, E-li-hu the son of Barachel the Bu-zite (Job chapters 32-37). After E-li-hu, Job was confronted by God because of his much speaking. In his answer, he acknowledged that he had spoken foolishly and decided to be silent from then.

*Behold, I am vile; what shall I answer thee? I will lay
mine hand upon my mouth.* (Job 40: 4)

What job went through was not easy. A lot of us would fail miserably at the first sets of afflictions that he suffered. The thing we have to learn here is to beware of self-pity because it was the giant that brought Job down to the level where he opened his mouth in defence of himself.

Jesus rejected self-pity

As the Lord Jesus was being led to Golgotha, a great company of people followed Him, and amongst the multitude were women that bewailed and lamented Him. This was the moment self-pity could have gotten hold of Him. Jesus, however, turned to them and said,

> . . . *Daughters of Jerusalem, weep not for me, but weep for yourselves, and for your children. For, behold, the days are comimg, in which they shall say, Blessed are the barren, and the wombs that never bare, and the paps which never gave suck. Then shall they begin to say to the mountains, Fall on us; and to the hills, Cover us. For if they do these to things in a green tree, what shall be done in the dry?*
> (Luke 23: 28-31)

The Lord did not receive the pity of the women that bewailed Him. Someone who comes to you in pity when you are in affliction is dangerous to your destiny. Such a one can inject self-pity into your heart concerning what you are facing. Make no mistake, sympathies are intended for good. However, the reality is, they are hardly helpful. At such trying times we need people who can encourage us to hope in the Lord. People who tell us that we'll make it, God will see us through and that with every temptation He makes a way of escape for us (I Corinthians 10: 13-14).

On Golgotha, before the Lord Jesus was crucified, He was given vinegar mingled with gall to drink. This, they that were crucifying Him did most probably in pity, to help ease His pain, but He would not receive it (Matthew 27: 33-34).

It was not until He knew that all things were accomplished that the scripture might be fulfilled, that He said, "*I thirst*". They filled a sponge with vinegar, put it on hyssop and put it to His lips. This time He received it, and said, "*It is finished*", and He bowed His head and gave up the ghost (John 19: 28-30).

Perseverance

It is required that we persevere till we reach the fulfilment of our destinies. There is no point entering into this race and stopping short of the end, for no reward is given such a one. The book of Hebrews, in chapter 12, teaches that—in order to make it to the end we have to fix our eyes on the Lord Jesus. Why we have to set our eyes on Him is because He is the beginning and the end of our faith. He is, therefore our hope.

> *Wherefore seeing we also are compassed about with so great a cloud of witnesses, let us lay aside every weight, and the sin which doth so easily beset us, and let us run*

with patience the race that is set before us, Looking unto Jesus the author and finisher of our faith; who for the joy that was set before him endured the cross, despising the shame, and is set down at the right hand of the throne of God. (Hebrews 12: 1-2)

The thing that makes our faith to hold is the joy that awaits us in the end. Unless we fix our eyes on the joy before us, we cannot endure in the present. The Lord, Himself, endured the cross because of the joy that awaited Him. We cannot do without hope. As soon as hope is lost, faith crumbles, and with it, fellowship with God, for without faith on one can please God.

We are surrounded by so many witnesses of saints who through faith persevered to the end. Paul, for instance, endured until he finished his cause. In his last letter to Timothy he testified concerning this, saying:

For I am now ready to be offered, and the time of my departure is at hand. I have fought a good fight, I have finished my course, I have kept the faith: Henceforth there is laid up for me a crown of righteousness, which the Lord, the righteous judge, shall give me at that day: and not to me only, but unto all them also that love his appearing. (II Timothy 4: 6-8)

What a blessed point to reach in one's destiny! Pray we all reach the point of fulfilment of our destinies.

Tribulations work patience

Seeing the importance of role that hope plays in bringing us to the end, we have to rejoice in tribulations. This is because the troubles we go through work patience in us and patience, in turn, works experience and experience works hope.

> *And not only so, but we glory in tribulations also: knowing that tribulation worketh patience; And patience, experience; and experience, hope: And hope maketh not ashamed; because the love of God is shed abroad in our hearts by the Holy Ghost which is given unto us.* (Romans 5: 3-5)

Those whose hope is in the Lord aren't made ashamed because of the love of God that is shed in their hearts. He shows mercy to thousands of them that love Him and keep His commandments (Exodus 20: 6). From Paul's letter to the Romans we are encouraged to keep persevering in tribulations.

> *The Spirit itself beareth witness with our spirit, that we are the children of God: And if children, then heirs; heirs of God, and joint-heirs with Christ; if so be that we suffer with him, that we may be also glorified together.*

For I reckon that the sufferings of this present time are *not worthy* to be compared *with the glory which shall be revealed in us.* (Romans 8: 16-18)

The manifestations of the sons of God (glory that shall be revealed in them) shall bring about the liberation of the entire creation. This outweighs, by far, the sufferings that we endure.

CHAPTER 3

The salt of the earth

One of the ways Jesus described His disciples is that they are the salt of the earth (Matthew 5: 13). This description of His body reveals her work in bringing healing and preservation of the earth.

Salt has various uses—It is a necessity for life (Job 6: 6)—In the Old Testament, a covenant of salt indicated faithfulness, dependability and durability—It was included in the offerings of the children of Israel (Leviticus 2: 13; Exodus 30: 35)—In times of war it was sown to make enemy land barren (Judges 9: 45)—Newborn babies were rubbed with salt (Ezekiel 16: 4)—Salt is today used mainly for purification, and seasoning and preservation of food.

What makes believers in the Lord Jesus Christ the salt of the earth is His life in them.

Seasoning

Salt is categorised with herbs in its use for enhancing flavour of food. In regard to the function of the Church, her seasoning comes from quality of living that is conformed to the image of Christ. The disciple is expected to make steady progress into becoming like Christ from the moment he (or she) is born again. From henceforth he (or she) must press on till no guile is found in his (or her) mouth.

> Let your speech be *always with grace, seasoned with salt, that ye may know how ye ought to answer every man.*
> (Colossians 4: 6)

In order that we offend not in speech, our words have to be seasoned with salt. What we say affect people around us in one way or the other. Death and life are in the power of the tongue (Proverbs 18: 21). Bitter words have such strong misery producing power! They embitter lives of people they are aimed at, break up communities, destroy relationships, devastate homes, wither lives, take blossom off childhood, and many others. Wrecking the whole world today is the power of negative speech! From this we must break away and speak words of life into the world, for out of the mouths of the righteous are wells of life.

If we are double tongued, it goes to show we are not of the kingdom. We cannot bless God and at the same time curse our fellow men, Out of the same fountain cannot come out bitter and sweet water.

True, the tongue cannot be tamed by man, but those that are in the Lord Jesus Christ have been given power to overcome all works of the flesh.

But the tongue can no man tame; it is an unruly evil, full of deadly poison. Therewith bless we God, even the Father; and therewith curse we men, which are made after the similitude of God. Out of the same mouth proceedeth blessing and cursing. My brethren, these things ought not so to be. Doth a fountain send forth at the same place sweet water *and bitter?*

Can the fig tree, my brethren, bear olive berries? Either a vine, figs? So can *no fountain both yield salt water and fresh. Who* is *a wise man and endued with knowledge among you? Let him shew out of a good conversation his works with meekness of wisdom. But if ye have bitter envying and strife in your hearts, glory not, and lie not against the truth. This wisdom descendeth not from above, but* is *earthly, sensual, devilish. For where envying and strife* is, *there* is *confusion and every evil work.* (James 3: 8-16).

Controlling of the tongue is not an option, but a must; otherwise we deceive our own selves. If we are not careful, we can be in the house of God without being of the kingdom. In the eyes of God, the works of those who fail to bridle their mouths are vain.

> *If any man among you seem to be religious, and bridleth not his tongue, but deceiveth his own heart, this man's religion is vain. Pure religion and undefiled before God and the Father is this, To visit the fatherless and widows in their affliction, and to keep himself unspotted from the world.* (James 1: 26-27)

In order to deal with the tongue, we have to follow it to its roots. The mouth speaks out of the abundance of the heart. Therefore, to cleanse our lips, we have to cleanse our hearts. Whosoever keeps his mouth and his tongue keeps himself from troubles (Proverbs 21: 23), and hence from being spotted by the world.

Pressing on to bear the nature of Him that birthed us into His kingdom, we, by pureness, peace, gentleness, longsuffering, mercy—are enabled to bless all around us.

> *But the wisdom that is from above is first pure, then peaceable, gentle,* and *easy to be intreated, full of mercy and good fruits, without partiality, and without hypocrisy.* (James 3: 17-18)

Disinfectant

Salt is used for purification of certain substances and as antiseptic. The whole earth was corrupted at the fall of man. God, in His plan of redemption, is restoring wholeness to His creation by what He is doing in the lives of His people. When the sons of God shall have been restored to wholeness spirit, soul, and body, creation shall also be set free from corruption.

> *For the earnest expectation of the creature waiteth for the manifestation of the sons of God. For the creature was made subject to vanity, not willingly, but by reason of him who hath subjected* the same *in hope, Because the creature itself also shall be delivered from the bondage of corruption into the glorious liberty of the children of God.*
> (Romans 19-21)

In the present, by spreading the gospel, we bring wholeness in the lives of those that receive the message, as well as healing and deliverance to many.

Preservation

This is to do with the power that holds all things together in and on the face of this earth. God is upholding all things by the word of His power (Hebrews 1: 3). His people are preservatives on this earth because His word indwells them. The Lord God called them out from the nations of the earth to be His vessels in carrying His oracles by which all things are preserved.

Therefore, to reject the word of God is to reject the power that is holding all things together on this earth. Considering the fact that the nations are rejecting God's counsel, it is not a wonder that nature is today unleashing its destructive force.

How we are salted

We are salted by the fire of persecutions and tribulations for righteousness' sake. It took a suffering saviour to bring salvation into this world—It also takes a suffering church to bring healing to the nations. Where persecutions cease, the Church dies. As soon as we begin to compromise with the world in order to escape persecution, we loose our saltiness. It is important to always remember that God forbade the children of Israel from offering to Him sacrifices without salt.

> *And every oblation of thy meat offering shalt thou season with salt; neither shalt thou suffer the salt of the covenant of thy God to be lacking from thy meat offering: with all thine offerings thou shalt offer salt.* (Leviticus 2: 13)

Likewise, salt must be included in us as we offer ourselves to God a living sacrifice. Bringing sacrifices that cost nothing is not acceptable to Him. The Lord Jesus teaches that if any man will come after Him, he has to take up his cross daily and follow Him.

> So likewise, whosoever he be of you that forsaketh not all that he hath, he cannot be my disciple. Salt is good: but if the salt have lost his savour, wherewith shall it be seasoned? It is neither fit for the land, nor yet for the dunghill; but men cast it out. He that hath ears to hear, let him hear. (Luke 14: 33-35)

If the Lord Jesus was killed for preaching the gospel of the kingdom, how can we, His servants, escape the suffering of the cross?

When men trample underfoot the authority of a church, it is as a consequence of her loosing her seasoning. The authority of a glorious church cannot be trampled underfoot because she is a force to recon with!

In summary, the following are some of the reasons the salt of the earth is loosing her saltiness today.

1. Departure from belief in the scripture.

    Where the authority of scripture is rejected in preference to reasoning, the foundation of a church is built on sand. Before we begin to wonder how this can happen, let us take for instance, the question if the assemblies we are attending are being built on the commandments of God. How many Christians today know the Ten Commandments and keep it? The vast majority of those that profess to believe in the Lord Jesus Christ today do not even know where to find the Ten Commandments in the Bible!

We must be warned that to claim to be in the Spirit while despising the Law and the prophets is far worse than unbelief. If the authority of the word of God is being disobeyed by those in His house, why should we expect the world to receive it? The speed at which the devil is destroying this generation is evidence that the salt is not savouring the earth.

The fact that many professing to be Christians are standing and watching powerlessly while the devil goes about his work of destruction with impunity, shows a disconnect with the power of the gospel. How can the power be revealed through people who have settled for a standard of life that is not built on the commandments of God?

If we reject or neglect the word of God, how can we be salted? Persecutions always arise because of the word (Matthew 13: 21), and stop with compromise with the world. Where there is no persecution the salt looses its saltiness.

2. Attack on the nature and character of God.

The very nature and character of God have come under serious attack right in His house! We have today men assuming titles that are reserved for God alone; such titles like "Reverend" and "Father". Only God deserves to be revered, not mortal man. The many who call themselves spiritual fathers to some in the kingdom are clearly going against the teaching of the Lord Jesus Christ. We are to call no man "father" because God is our Father (Matthew 23: 9).

Moreover many leaders are today attacking God's office by usurping authorities that exclusively belong to God the Father, Son and the Holy Ghost. To demand unquestioned obedience is to claim equality with God. There is no authority that has been given to man that cannot be questioned. Only God exercises sovereign authority, that is, authority that is never to be questioned. What makes the positions of leaders that exercise sovereign authority different from that in which Satan fell?—For he said in his heart:

. . . , *I will ascend into heaven, I will exalt my throne above the stars of God: I will sit also upon the mount of the congregation, in the sides of the north: I will ascend above*

the heights of the clouds; I will be like the most High.
(Isaiah 14: 13-14)

There is great danger in following leadership that have set themselves above the congregations of God's people! Exaltation of leaders begins with simple things, such as preparation of special seats for them. In some assemblies the seats set aside for leaders are like thrones! The Lord Jesus teaches us to loath the love of salutations, going about in special clothing, and chief seats in our assemblies and in feasts.

And he said unto them in his doctrine, Beware of the scribes, which love to go in long clothing, and love *salutations in the marketplaces, And the chief seats in the synagogues, and the uppermost rooms at feasts: Which devour widows' houses, and for a pretence make long prayers: these shall receive greater damnation.* (Mark 12: 38-40)

The idea of special seats for ministers and elders is certainly not from the word of God. With God there is no respect person. The first people to come into the assembly should take the front seats. If leaders are late, let them take the back seats like everyone else.

Love of salutations leads to acceptance of worship. This is evident today in the practice of some leadership in their receipt of worship from the people they lead! We see in the scripture that when saints mistakenly worshiped angels or servants of God, the intended worships were not received. We see in Revelation 19: 10 and 22: 8-9 that when John fell down at the feet of the angel to worship, the latter told him not to.

Peter told Cornelius not to fall at his feet to worship because he was mortal man (Acts 10: 25-26). Likewise Paul and Barnabas did not receive the worships of the people of Lystra that wanted to offer sacrifices to them, supposing that they were gods (Acts 14: 14-15).

Love of special clothing is motivated by desire to stand out in the congregation, which is actually pride. If our Lord and Master did not clothe Himself conspicuously amongst His disciples, who are we to seek to be different? We know that the Lord did not look any different from His disciples in appearance from the fact that Judas had to kiss Him, to identify Him to the soldiers that arrested Him (Mark 14: 44). Yet, sadly, it does not take much to find out who the leaders are in many assemblies today!

The Lord's calling upon His servants does not enthrone them amongst His people. He is their King and Lord. His ministers are, but servants of the people.

3. Attack on the Lord Jesus Christ.

By taking blasphemous titles many leaders are snaring God's people. In mentioning the titles the people blaspheme! An example of such titles is "Vicar". It is a title that takes the place of Christ. Being an abbreviation from the title "Vicarious Filii Dei" it means "one who stands in the place of—the Son of—God". It is, therefore, an attempt to replace the leadership at the head of the Church, even the position of the Lord Jesus Christ!

The responsibility is on us to find out the meanings of titles before we use them to address people. Particularly titles that cannot be found in the scripture, we must check out, lest we blaspheme in using them.

Moreover, many are claiming the position of the Lord Jesus by trying to operate in all the five offices of the fivefold ministry. Only Christ operates in all the five offices. He is an apostle, a prophet, an evangelist, a pastor and a teacher. After He had led captivity captive, He gave gifts to men to continue the work of the kingdom; giving some to be apostles, some prophets, some evangelists, some pastors, and some teachers. Their work is to perfect the saints and prepare them for the work of the ministry (Ephesians 4: 8-12).

Clearly, the Lord has not given anyone of His servants to operate in all the five offices of the fivefold ministry. Those that set themselves to solely lead err by taking the position of Christ. As a consequence, assemblies that are built on ministries of sole individuals operate under antichrist spirit. The term "antichrist" doesn't only mean "against Christ", but also "in the position of Christ".

In conclusion, where the authority of scripture is rejected, and the nature and character of God is under attack, the Church looses all that is central to her faith, and consequently her saltiness.

CHAPTER 4

The light of the world

The Lord Jesus said in His description of His disciples as the light of the world:

> *Ye are the light of the world. A city that is set on an hill cannot be hid. Neither do men light a candle, and put it under a bushel, but on a candlestick; and it giveth light unto all that are in the house. Let your light so shine before men, that they may see your good works, and glorify your Father which is in heaven.* (Matthew 5: 14-16)

Our light shines before men when they see our good works and glorify our Father in heaven.

We are the light of the world because Christ lives in us. The light that is in us is the brightness of the glory of God in the life of His son Jesus Christ (Hebrews 1: 2-3). Out of darkness we have been called into Christ's marvellous light so that we may show forth His praise on the earth (I Peter 2: 9).

The calling upon us to be the light of the world focuses on our ministry in acts of kindness to our fellow men. We have been called to minister love to all, particularly bringing hope to those that have been battered and bruised due to the consequences of wrong choices in their lives, by calamities, as well as due to the injustices in the systems of this world.

A city set on a hill cannot be hid

There are forces that try to contend to obscure our light, but thankfully they have never succeeded. When one's light begins to shine through good works, surprisingly there are people, even within the house of God, who will try to oppose or obscure it. Many brethren have been hurt and discouraged from their ministries by such forces.

The Lord is giving us a solid fact on which to stand and fight discouragement. The shinning of our light is as sure as the fact that a city that is built on a hill cannot be hid. Also we see in Isaiah 58: 8 and 10, that if we obey the voice of the Lord to minister love to the needy, our light shall rise in obscurity and break forth as the morning; and as bright as the noon day.

And if *thou draw out thy soul to the hungry, and satisfy the afflicted soul; then shall thy light rise in obscurity, and thy darkness* be *as the noonday:* (Isaiah 58: 10)

Just as the breaking forth of the morning and the brightness of noonday cannot be stopped, so is the shining of our light.

Let your light so shine

The fact that we are commanded to let our light so shine means that,

1. We are not to hinder it from shining.
2. We are to abound in good works.

THE HINDRANCE

It is we, by ourselves, that can hinder our light from shining. The hindrance comes from the carnal nature, for it is self-centred. Unless we are delivered from self-centeredness, we cannot reach out in kindness to others and as a consequence, our light won't shine.

The question is, how can we be delivered from self-centredness if we are not urgent in dealing with the carnal nature? From the book of Acts and the epistles, we see that the early church dealt with the carnal nature **urgently and swiftly**. Time and again we see that those that were converted to the Lord were baptised in water, and got filled and baptised in the Holy Ghost the same days of their conversions. For instance, as Peter shared the word with the house of Cornelius, the Holy Spirit fell on them and they were baptised.

It is important to note the fact that they received the baptism of the Spirit and that of water the same day (Acts 10: 34-48).

Also we read in Acts chapter 8: 14-17 that when the apostles from Jerusalem heard that Samaria had received the word of God, they wasted no time in sending them help so that they might receive the Holy Ghost—for as yet, they had only received water baptism. Peter and John went and laid hands on the Samaritan believers and they received the Holy Ghost and were baptised in Him.

If we are not urgent in seeking to receive both water baptism and that of the Spirit, how can we overcome the carnal nature? We must understand that both baptisms are important in overcoming the works of the flesh. In water baptism we make a public declaration that we have been buried with Christ and that we are rising out of the water to live a new life in Him. In baptism of the Holy Spirit we are totally surrendered to God. Paul said to the Galatians, "This *I say then, Walk in the Spirit, and ye shall not fulfil the lust of the flesh.*" (Galatians 5: 16). Clearly, the ultimate deathblow to our carnal nature is dealt by the fire of the Holy Ghost.

WHY WE MUST ABOUND IN GOOD WORKS

We must abound in good works and alms deeds because we need them to keep our lamps burning (keep our faith alive). True, we are not saved (justified) because of good works, but they are part of the proof of the work of sanctification in our lives. Included in the will of God for us are also acts of love that we are to do to our fellow men. Good works (acts of kindness) are part of the fruit of the Spirit in us. We must be warned that if our faith be dead, that is, without works, we cannot inherit the kingdom of heaven.

What doth it profit, my brethren, though a man say he hath faith, and have not works? can faith save him? If a brother or sister be naked, and destitute of daily food, And one of you say unto them, Depart in peace, be ye warmed and filled; notwithstanding ye give them not those things which are needful to the body; what doth it profit? Even so faith, if it hath not works, is dead, being alone. Yea, a man may say, Thou hast faith, and I have works: shew me thy faith without thy works, and I will shew thee my faith by my works. Thou believest that there is one God; thou doest well: the devils also believe, and tremble. But wilt thou know, O vain man, that faith without works is dead? (James 2: 14-19)

For as the body without the spirit is dead, so faith without works is dead also. (James 2: 26)

Love is expressed in the action it prompts. Through good works and alms deeds we show that we have the nature of God in us, for he who abides in love abides in God and God in him (I John 4:16).

From the parable of the ten virgins we learn how the five foolish ones missed the kingdom because they did not have enough oil to keep their lamps burning (Matthew 25: 1-12). This clearly shows us why it is important for us to abound in acts of kindness towards our fellow men—which brings us to the all important question concerning this subject.

Have we reserve of oil for our lamps?

This is the question we'd be wise to answer now rather than when it is too late. In the present we can do something about it. The reason we must abound in good works is that we may have reserve of oil for our lamps. Tabitha (Dorcas), for instance, had buckets and buckets of oil reserved for her lamp. She was so full of good works and alms deeds that when she died, the widows she had helped stood by her body weeping, showing all the coats and garments she had made for them.

> *Now there was at Joppa a certain disciple named Tabitha,*
> *which by interpretation is called Dorcas: this woman was*
> *full of good works and almsdeeds which she did. And it*
> *came to pass in those days, that she was sick, and died:*

whom when they had washed, they laid her *in an upper chamber. And forasmuch as Lydda was nigh to Joppa, and the disciples had heard that Peter was there, they sent unto him two men, desiring* him *that he would not delay to come to them. Then Peter arose and went with them. When he was come, they brought him into the upper chamber: and all the widows stood by him weeping, and shewing the coats and garments which Dorcas made, while she was with them.* (Acts 9: 36-39)

Do we have good works and alms deeds that can follow us like those of Tabitha? If we have caused the hearts of the poor and the needy to bless God because of His provisions for them through our hands, then we are blessed indeed. Otherwise we must urgently cry out to God so that we may become compassionate and extend our hands to help those in need before it is too late for us.

We cannot afford to take comfort in few acts of kindness because they cannot keep our lamps burning. From the parable of the ten virgins we see how the oil in the lamps of the five foolish virgins soon burnt out. Because they had no reservoir of oil for refilling their lamps, they missed the kingdom (Matthew 25: 1-12). The fact that they were virgins (pure) did not count because their light could not shine. Therefore, we cannot afford to concentrate our efforts on our spiritual wellbeing while ignoring the need to reach out to others in kindness.

It'll be foolish of us if we wait until the Bridegroom is at the door and then begin looking to buy enough oil for our lamps. Acts of love cannot be borrowed or shared with our fellow brethren; neither can they be done in a few moments. It takes time to cultivate love. The time those that wait to the last moment to buy oil return to the banquet, the door will have been shut. When they knock, the Lord will declare to them that He does not know them. Pray this will not be our case.

CHAPTER 5

The Law and the Prophets

The Lord Jesus dealt with the issue of the Law and the prophets straight away as He laid the foundation of the kind of life His disciples ought to live. He said that He did not come to do away with them, but to fulfil.

> *Think not that I am come to destroy the law, or the*
> *prophets: I am not come to destroy but to fulfil. For verily*
> *I say unto you, Till heaven and earth pass, one jot or one*
> *tittle shall in no wise pass from the law, till all be fulfilled.*
> (Matthew 5: 17-18)

The Lord Jesus puts the whole scripture under the Law and the prophets. We learn from Revelation 19: 3 that He is also called the Word. Therefore, from Genesis to Revelation the scripture testifies of Him; and the testimony of Jesus is the spirit of prophecy (Revelation 19: 10). The Lord threw more light on this when He expounded the scripture to two of His disciples that He joined as they walked from Jerusalem to Emmaus.

In the account in Luke 24: 13-33, the day the Lord Jesus was resurrected from the dead, He appeared to two of His disciples that were journeying to Emmaus, from Jerusalem. As the two went along sorrowing concerning the things that had happened to Him, He asked them the reason for their sadness. After they had explained to Him why, He rebuked them for being slow of heart to believe all that the prophets had spoken. He then expounded to them in all the scriptures the things about Himself—Beginning from Moses (Genesis, Exodus, Leviticus, Numbers, and Deuteronomy) and all the prophets (form Joshua to Malachi).

All of scripture is given us that we may learn to fear God and repent of our ways and obey the Law.

> *For whatsoever things were written aforetime were written for our learning, that we through patience and comfort of the scriptures might have hope.* (Romans 15: 4)

- The Prophets prophesied in hope that Israel and the nations of the world would repent and obey the Law.
- The gospels are recordings of the fulfilment of the Law and the prophets in the Lord Jesus Christ.

- The epistles are teachings and admonisions to us to obey the Law.
- In the book of Revelation is revealed the reward of the righteous for obeying the voice of the Lord, and the judgement of the disobedient for not keeping the Law.

The Law is God's instruction to His people in righteousness. What can be wrong with that? He who receives instruction is preserved, but he who doesn't is destroyed. Examples are given us of individuals, and nations that were blessed because they obeyed God's voice; and of those that were destroyed for not obeying His word.

> *Now all these things happened unto them for ensamples: and they are written for our admonition, upon whom the ends of the world are come.* (I Corinthians 10: 11)

One of the biggest attacks on the Church today is the doctrine that teaches that New Testament believers are not under the Law, but in the Spirit. True, Paul said in his letter to the Galatians, in chapter 5: 18 that if we be led of the Spirit, we are not under the Law. However, we have to be careful to interpret this verse of scripture in context. Alarmingly, many in the house of God today have mistaken Galatians 5: 18 to mean that they are above the authority of the Law. Some are even inclined to think that the keeping of the Law kills, when actually it does the exact opposite.

The Lord commands us to listen to Him and obey His voice that it may be well with us and with our children (Deuteronomy 6: 17-18; Jeremiah 11: 1-8). There is nothing wrong with the Law. To the Romans Paul wrote concerning the Law and the commandments, saying:

> *Wherefore the law is holy, and the commandment holy, and just, and good.* (Romans 7: 12)

In Romans 6: 14, he said:

> *For sin shall not have dominion over you: for ye are not under the law, but under grace.*

We have to be careful here to understand that the work of the Law is included in that of grace. In context, we see that Paul was admonishing the Romans about not yielding their members to sin because they were not under the Law, but grace. This is because the power to overcome the sinful nature is not given in the Law, but under grace.

True, Paul said that the Law was/is weak through the flesh (Romans 8: 3), but before we begin despising it for this reason, let us take time understand what Paul meant. He was clear in his explanation that it was the sinful nature (the law of sin and death) that corrupted the soul of man at the fall that was the problem, **not the Law**! The sinful nature is always provoked by restraint because it doesn't like to be restrained. Therefore, it resists the Law such that it makes it difficult for us to obey the voice of the Lord.

For I know that in me (that is, in my flesh,) dwelleth no good thing: for to will is present with me; but how *to perform that which is good I find not. For the good that I would I do not: but the evil which I would not, that I do.*

Now if I do that I would not, it is no more I that do it, but sin that dwelleth in me. I find then a law, that, when I would do good, evil is present with me. For I delight in the law of God after the inward man:

But I see another law in my members, warring against the law of my mind, and bringing me into captivity to the law of sin which is in my members. O wretched man that I am! who shall deliver me from the body of this death? I thank God through Jesus Christ our Lord. So then with the mind I myself serve the law of God; but with the flesh the law of sin. (Romans 7: 18-25)

For the flesh lusteth against the Spirit, and the Spirit against the flesh: and these are contrary the one to the other: so that ye cannot do the things that ye would. (Galatians 5: 17)

What is fighting man to stop him from obeying the voice of the Lord is within him. It was hard for Old Testament saints to overcome the sinful nature because they were not given the power to overcome it. On the other hand, New Testament saints can, if they obey the word of the Lord, walk in total victory over the sinful nature because they've been given the power to overcome it (John 1: 12).

Clearly, in the New Testament, saints are given more than those in the Old Testament. There is, therefore, no reason for those that are in the New Testament to boast over those in the Old.

The shocking, and at the same time sad thing about those that boast of not being under the Law is the fact that—the vast majority of them are actually as fleshly as the world in their ways. To put it bluntly, they are anti-Semitic and spiritual anarchists. Before you say, wait a minute; please define for yourself what it means to be without the Law—isn't it LAWLESSNESS?

The covenants

Generally speaking, a covenant is an agreement between two parties, the terms and conditions of which if kept, brings blessings on them and punishment if violated.

In the Law are the terms and conditions of both covenants that God made with His people. He gave them to Israel the first time in the covenant that He made with them on Mount Sinai amidst thundering, fire, lightening and smoke. Israel promised to perform all the words that God spoke to them.

> *And Moses came and told the people all the words of the*
> *LORD, and all the judgments: and all the people answered*
> *with one voice, and said, All the words which the LORD*
> *hath said will we do.* (Exodus 24: 3)

However, right at the foot of Mount Sinai the people broke the covenant. When they saw that Moses had delayed to come down from the Mount, for he was there forty days and forty nights (Exodus 24: 18), they made a golden calf and worshiped it. In judgement, 3000 men were killed by the Levites at the command of Moses. As a consequence, eleven tribes of Israel lost the priesthood. From then on it was only the tribe of Levi that could perform work in the priestly office. God's original plan was, and is, to have the whole nation of Israel priests unto Him in the earth (Exodus 19: 4-6).

Time and again Israel broke the covenant in their generations and suffered the consequences.

> *When he slew them, then they sought him: and they returned*
> *and enquired early after God. And they remembered that*
> *God* was *their rock, and the high God their redeemer.*
> *Nevertheless they did flatter him with their mouth,*
> *and they lied unto him with their tongues.*

95

For their heart was not right with him, neither were they stedfast in his covenant. But he, being full of compassion, forgave their iniquity, and destroyed them not: yea, many a time turned he his anger away, and did not stir up all his wrath.

For he remembered that they were but flesh; a wind that passeth away, and cometh not again. (Psalms 78: 34-39)

In contrast, God does not break His promises. His oath to raise up children to Abraham that will walk in His ways is everlasting. Although Israel broke His covenant, in mercy He remembered that they were flesh, and promised to make with them a new covenant, based on better promises. This covenant, unlike the old one, **would give them power to overcome their flesh so that they may walk in His commands**. The New Testament is the new covenant that God promised to make with Israel. He said through Prophet Jeremiah:

Behold, the days come, saith the LORD, that I will make a new covenant with the house of Israel, and with the house of Judah:

Not according to the covenant that I made with their fathers in the day that *I took them by the hand to bring them out of the land of Egypt; which my covenant they brake, although I was an husband unto them, saith the LORD:*

> *But this* shall be *the covenant that I will make with*
> *the house of Israel; After those days, saith the LORD, I*
> *will put my law in their inward parts, and write it in*
> *their hearts; and will be their God, and they shall be my*
> *people.*
>
> *And they shall teach no more every man his neighbour,*
> *and every man his brother, saying, Know the LORD:*
> *for they shall all know me, from the least of them unto*
> *the greatest of them, saith the LORD: for I will forgive*
> *their iniquity, and I will remember their sin no more.*
> (Jeremiah 31: 31-34)

It is important to take note of two things in the above passage.

1. The New Covenant was promised to the house of Israel,
    and the house of Judah. This shows us clearly that God
    made the New Testament with Israel. Gentile believers, as
    we understand in the book of Romans in chapter 11, **were**
    grafted into it. The Lord Jesus started His church with
    Jews; we can't change that, nor question Him why.

    > *For who hath known the mind of the Lord? or who hath*
    > *been his counsellor?* (Romans 11: 34)

Rather, gentile believers should be grateful to God for grafting
them into the New Covenant. To attempt to separate Israel from
the New Testament is to attempt to exclude them from the faith

of their forefather Abraham through his seed Jesus Christ (Yeshua HaMashiach). In other words, it is an attempt to exclude them from what is theirs!

The Lord Jesus said that salvation is of the Jews (John 4: 22). God chose Israel to be His vessel through whom He brought into effect His plan of salvation for mankind.

We must beware of the fact that presenting the message of the gospel to Jews with an attitude of spiritual superiority is arrogance. To put it bluntly, it is anti-Semitism and Replacement Theology in disguise. The scripture gives gentile believers a stern warning not to boast against Israel. The most common form of boasting today is in the claim of those that say they are in the Spirit, but reject the Law.

We have to understand that the New Testament does not do away with the Law, but establishes it.

They that reject the Law are high-minded, thinking they are more spiritual than those that keep it. The scripture warns that such people are in unbelief and shall be cut off from where they have been grafted into the good olive tree. We receive the goodness of the Lord only if we continue in the faith through grace, and the work of grace does not despise or do away with the Law.

Boast not against the branches. But if thou boast, thou bearest not the root, but the root thee. Thou wilt say then, The branches were broken off, that I might be graffed in. Well; because of unbelief they were broken off, and thou standest by faith. Be not highminded, but fear:

For if God spared not the natural branches, take heed *lest he also spare not thee. Behold therefore the goodness and severity of God: on them which fell, severity; but toward thee, goodness, if thou continue in* his *goodness: otherwise thou also shalt be cut off.*

And they also, if they abide not still in unbelief, shall be graffed in: for God is able to graff them in again.

For if thou wert cut out of the olive tree which is wild by nature, and wert graffed contrary to nature into a good olive tree: how much more shall these, which be the natural branches, *be graffed into their own olive tree?* (Romans 11: 18-24)

We stand in the faith in Christ by grace, therefore, let us fear and walk in humility, regarding the Lord's body, of which we are part, **with Israel**.

2. The second thing we learn from Jeremiah 31: 31-34 is that the terms and conditions of the New Covenant (Testament) are written on the tablets of the hearts of God's people. Problem solved! God has not done away

with the Law in the New Testament, but writes it on the tablets of the hearts of His people.

The purpose of the Law

The Law is there to show us how we have transgressed God's standard of holiness. In other words, the Law is, as it were, the doctor. It gives the diagnosis of the problems in our lives showing us how we have fallen short of the glory of God.

> *Whosoever committeth sin transgresseth also the law: for sin is the transgression of the law.* (I John 3: 4)

I John 5: 17 teaches that all unrighteousness is sin. Unless we understand that sin is the transgression of the Law, we won't be convicted. The Law is there to show us our transgressions, that we may realise our need for salvation and, therefore, a redeemer.

> *Now we know that what things soever the law saith, it saith to them who are under the law: that every mouth may be stopped, and all the world may become guilty before God.* (Romans 3: 19)

We have to be careful to understand that the above scripture is not saying the Law is for those who were/are in the Old Testament. In context, we see that this verse is saying—it is those that submit to (rank under) the Law that can obey its commands. In other words, the Law speaks to or is received by those that humble themselves and submit to it. Those that reject its message cannot be convicted of their sins. How can we be convicted of sin if we do not know what it is? Paul said he had not known sin, but by the Law.

> *What shall we say then? Is the law sin? God forbid. Nay, I had not known sin, but by the law: for I had not known lust, except the law had said, Thou shalt not covet. But sin, taking occasion by the commandment, wrought in me all manner of concupiscence. For without the law sin was dead.* (Romans 7: 7).

From the above verse of scripture it is clear that it was the Law that helped Paul to realise how he had sinned and fallen short of the glory of God. He recognised the importance of the Law in bringing man to the point of awareness of his transgressions against God's standard of holiness. Clear enough—reject the Law, and you'll never know how you are sinning against God. Call it what you may, but the fact remains that it is not by the leading of the Spirit of God, for He will never lead anyone to despise or reject the Law.

We must be warned that rejection of the Law is lawlessness (practice of iniquity). Therefore, those that are arrogant against the Law are doing so to their own detriment. True, without the Law there is no knowledge of sin. The question is, shall we then reject the Law so that we may not be aware of sin? Not so! The fact is, choosing to be ignorant of the Law or rejecting it does not do away with the consequences of sin.

Before the Law, sin was in the world, but was not imputed. Nevertheless, this did not excuse man from the consequences of sin. Death was present in him to always lead him to do that which destroyed him (Romans 5: 13-14). This was/is the law of sin and death (sinful nature) which was written in man at the fall of man.

Present within us is a corruption that pushes us to go against the will of God, leading to that which destroys. Paul found out this fact the hard way though the struggles he had within him. He said:

> For we know that the law is spiritual: but I am carnal, sold under sin. For that which I do I allow not: for what I would, that do I not; but what I hate, that do I. If then I do that which I would not, I consent unto the law that it is good.
>
> Now then it is no more I that do it, but sin that dwelleth in me.
>
> For I know that in me (that is, in my flesh,) dwelleth no good thing: for to will is present with me; but how to perform that which is good I find not. For the good that I would I do not: but the evil which I would not, that I do.

Now if I do that I would not, it is no more I that do it,
but sin that dwelleth in me. I find then a law, that, when
I would do good, evil is present with me.

For I delight in the law of God after the inward man:
But I see another law in my members, warring against the
law of my mind, and bringing me into captivity to the law
of sin which is in my members. (Romans 7: 14-23)

The things that Paul wanted to do in righteousness, he could not do. Instead he obeyed the will of his flesh in doing what the Law of God forbade him. Form this, he realised that something within him, which he called the law within his member, was pushing him to do wrong. He struggled until he found out that the solution to this problem was/is in walking according to the leading of the Spirit.

There is *therefore now no condemnation to them which*
are in Christ Jesus, who walk not after the flesh, but
after the Spirit. For the law of the Spirit of life in Christ
Jesus hath made me free from the law of sin and death.
(Romans 8: 1-2)

All of us, without exception, can identify with Paul in the struggle between the flesh and the working of the Spirit in us. Paul, in his explanation, has helped us to understand how we can walk in total victory over the sinful nature.

> This *I say then, Walk in the Spirit, and ye shall not fulfil the lust of the flesh. For the flesh lusteth against the Spirit, and the Spirit against the flesh: and these are contrary the one to the other: so that ye cannot do the things that ye would.* (Galatians 5: 16-17)

We have to recognise the fact that the war between the flesh and the Spirit is raging in us twenty four hours of every day of our lives. The result of which is, we are either obeying our flesh or the Spirit of God. To solve this problem, we have to deal a death blow to our fleshly nature. The power to overcome the sinful (fleshly) nature was given us, through grace, when we received the Lord Jesus Christ (Yeshua HaMashiach).

> *But as many as received him, to them gave he power to become the sons of God,* even *to them that believe on his name:* (John 1: 12)

Through the atoning work of the blood of the Lamb we are justified and given power to become the sons of God. This means when we are justified we are given power to be conformed into the image of the Lord Jesus Christ.

> *For whom he did foreknow, he also did predestinate* to be *conformed to the image of his Son, that he might be the firstborn among many brethren* (Romans 8: 29).

JUSTIFICATION

It is important to understand that justification is by grace, through faith, not of works.

> *For by grace are ye saved through faith; and that not of yourselves:* it is *the gift of God: Not of works, lest any man should boast.* (Ephesians 2: 8-9)

No flesh can be justified by keeping the Law. The Law is there to show us our transgressions so that we may be convicted and come to repentance. It is important to understand that under both covenants (the Old and the New Testaments) saints were/ are not justified because of keeping the Law. They were/are saved because the Law convicted them of their sins and as a result they repented.

> *Therefore by the deeds of the law there shall no flesh be justified in his sight: for by the law* is *the knowledge of sin. But now the righteousness of God without the law is manifested, being witnessed by the law and the prophets; Even the righteousness of God* which is *by faith of Jesus Christ unto all and upon all them that believe: for there is no difference: For all have sinned, and come short of the glory of God;* (Romans 3: 20-23)

For us to be saved, it is necessary that we repent of our sins. We have to be careful to understand that keeping of the Law without breaking before God in contrition doesn't do any good. It only shows trust in oneself for righteousness. The Lord Jesus shows us this fact clearly in the parable of two men that went into the temple to pray.

> *And he spake this parable unto certain which trusted in themselves that they were righteous, and despised others: Two men went up into the temple to pray; the one a Pharisee, and the other a publican.*
>
> *The Pharisee stood and prayed thus with himself, God, I thank thee, that I am not as other men* are, *extortioners, unjust, adulterers, or even as this publican. I fast twice in the week, I give tithes of all that I possess.*
>
> *And the publican, standing afar off, would not lift up so much as* his *eyes unto heaven, but smote upon his breast, saying, God be merciful to me a sinner.*
>
> *I tell you, this man went down to his house justified* rather *than the other: for every one that exalteth himself shall be abased; and he that humbleth himself shall be exalted.* (Luke 18: 9-14)

The Pharisee narrated to God his good deeds in comparison to the deeds of others, including those of the publican who was praying at the same time. Although he had kept the Law, he did it to attain righteousness by himself! He did not keep the Law as a result of inward change in his life due to repentance and the consequent forgiveness of his sins. In other words, he did not depend on the grace of God to save him.

The publican, on the other hand, sought the grace of God in prayers. Standing afar off, he couldn't even lift up his eyes to heaven, but beat on his chest, saying, *God be merciful to me a sinner.*

Of the two men, the publican went home justified while the Pharisee wasn't.

In summary—We are justified freely by God's grace through the redemption that is in Christ Jesus. Notice, though, in order for us to be justified, we have to repent of our sins—To be able to repent of our sins, we have to break before God in contrition—To be contrite we have to be convicted of our sins—In order to be convicted of our sins, we need the Law to show us how we have transgressed God's standard of holiness. Are there alternative ways of reaching justification? The answer is, absolutely none!

It is those that believe in God, and in contrition seek His forgiveness of their transgressions, that are justified. Abraham depended on the mercies of God, not his own works, to justify him from all ungodliness.

What shall we say then that Abraham our father, as pertaining to the flesh, hath found? For if Abraham were justified by works, he hath whereof *to glory; but not before God. For what saith the scripture? Abraham believed God, and it was counted unto him for righteousness. Now to him that worketh is the reward not reckoned of grace, but of debt. But to him that worketh not, but believeth on him that justifieth the ungodly, his faith is counted for righteousness.* (Romans 4: 1-5)

It was Abraham's belief that God, in His mercy, justifies the ungodly that was counted to him for righteousness. He is, therefore, father of all who believe in God and depend on His mercy to forgive them; both Jews and gentiles.

Being justified freely by his grace through the redemption that is in Christ Jesus: Whom God hath set forth to be a propitiation through faith in his blood, to declare his righteousness for the remission of sins that are past, through the forbearance of God;

To declare, I say, at this time his righteousness: that he might be just, and the justifier of him which believeth in Jesus. Where is boasting then? It is excluded. By what law? of works? Nay: but by the law of faith.

Therefore we conclude that a man is justified by faith without the deeds of the law. Is he the God of the Jews only? is he not also of the Gentiles? Yes, of the Gentiles also:

Seeing it is one God, which shall justify the circumcision by faith, and uncircumcision through faith.

Do we then make void the law through faith? God forbid: yea, we establish the law. (Romans 3: 24-30)

Grace establishes the law

In conclusion, we must understand that the work of grace establishes the Law in us by enabling us to fulfill its righteousness. If we remain in the Lord Jesus Christ, we'll be able to walk in total victory over sin, for in Him our flesh is crucified. Paul testified to this, saying:

> *I am crucified with Christ: nevertheless I live; yet not I, but Christ liveth in me: and the life which I now live in the flesh I live by the faith of the Son of God, who loved me, and gave himself for me.* (Galatians 2: 20)

Clearly, we are able to crucify the flesh only if we are in the Lord Jesus Christ. Outside of Him, we can't. He defeated the works of the flesh in His body so that those that are in Him can walk in ultimate victory over sin.

CHAPTER 6

The Law of the Spirit

The Law of the Spirit of life in Christ Jesus makes us free from the law of sin and death (Romans 8: 2). We must be careful to recognise that it is not the **Law of Moses** that we are freed from, but the law of sin and death that is within us. If we do not get this right away, we'll be sitting ducks for the "Faith Movement".

It is important for us to understand that a covenant always has terms and conditions without which it cannot come into effect. The terms and conditions of the Old Testament are given in the Law, written on two tablets of stone and in a book. Those of the New Testament are in the Law written on the tablets of the hearts of God's people.

It is also important for us to understand that the two covenants (the Old and the New Testaments) were ratified in blood. The reasons being, for sinful man to come into covenant with God, there is a necessity for atonement of his sins. Without the shedding of blood, there is no forgiveness of sin.

> *For where a testament is, there must also of necessity be the death of the testator. For a testament is of force after men are dead: otherwise it is of no strength at all while the testator liveth. Whereupon neither the first testament was dedicated without blood.*
>
> *For when Moses had spoken every precept to all the people according to the law, he took the blood of calves and of goats, with water, and scarlet wool, and hyssop, and sprinkled both the book, and all the people, Saying, This is the blood of the testament which God hath enjoined unto you. Moreover he sprinkled with blood both the tabernacle, and all the vessels of the ministry.* (Hebrews 9: 16-21)

To ratify the Old Covenant, Moses sprinkled both the people and the book of the Law with the blood of oxen slain for the dedication of the agreement (Exodus 24: 5-8).

The New Covenant came into effect when the Lord Jesus shed His blood on the cross at Golgotha. He had said to His disciples at the Passover meal before His suffering and death, "*This cup is the new testament in my blood, which is shed for you*" (Luke 22: 20). His blood was shed for the remission of sin so that man could come into covenant relationship with God. Sin that separated us from God, He has atoned for, and has thus made a way for us to reach God through His own righteousness that has been imparted to us.

Unless we understand that both covenants are agreements between God and His people upon the condition that they keep His commands, we'll miss the kingdom. To reject the Law is to effectively prove that one is not in covenant relationship with God; for it is by keeping His commandments that we abide in Him and Him in us.

> *Beloved, if our heart condemn us not,* then *have we confidence toward God. And whatsoever we ask, we receive of him, because we keep his commandments, and do those things that are pleasing in his sight. And this is his commandment, That we should believe on the name of his Son Jesus Christ, and love one another, as he gave us commandment. And he that keepeth his commandments dwelleth in him, and he in him. And hereby we know that he abideth in us, by the Spirit which he hath given us.* (I John 3: 21-24)

Clearly, the proof that Christ abides in us is in keeping of His commandments. Should any question arise due to the fact that the above scripture is teaching that the commandment of God is that we should believe on Christ, and to love one another as Christ has commanded us, the answer is right within. To believe on Christ is to keep the Law, for He empowers those who are in Him to fulfil the righteousness of the Law.

> *For what the law could not do, in that it was weak through the flesh, God sending his own Son in the likeness of sinful flesh, and for sin, condemned sin in the flesh: That the righteousness of the law might be fulfilled in us, who walk not after the flesh, but after the Spirit.* (Romans 8: 3-4)

When we walk in love, we fulfil the Law and the prophets.

> *Owe no man any thing, but to love one another: for he that loveth another hath fulfilled the law. For this, Thou shalt not commit adultery, Thou shalt not kill, Thou shalt not steal, Thou shalt not bear false witness, Thou shalt not covet; and if there be any other commandment, it is briefly comprehended in this saying, namely, Thou shalt love thy neighbour as thyself. Love worketh no ill to his neighbour: therefore love is the fulfilling of the law.* Romans 13: 8-10)

To whom much is given, much is also required

The Lord Jesus expounds on how more is expected of saints in the New Testament than those in the Old in the fact that the Law is expanded in the New Testament to include its violation in the mind and heart of the worshiper.

MURDER

In the Old Covenant murder was imputed when it was committed literally. In the New Covenant, however, murder begins in the heart with hatred, wrath, bitterness, resentfulness, withdrawal, and all other forms of un-forgiveness. The Lord explains this, saying:

> *Ye have heard that it was said by them of old time, Thou shalt not kill; and whosoever shall kill shall be in danger of the judgment: But I say unto you, That whosoever is angry with his brother without a cause shall be in danger of the judgment: and whosoever shall say to his brother, Raca, shall be in danger of the council: but whosoever shall say, Thou fool, shall be in danger of hell fire.* Matthew 5: 21-22)

Anger without cause, saying to someone Ra-ca (vain person or doomed to mount to nothing), and calling one a fool, all mount to murder in the New Covenant. Murder that is committed in the heart originates from taking of offences. It is upon each of us to save ourselves from this sin, because offences will always come. In seeking reconciliation swiftly we give no chance to murder, otherwise our prayers won't be answered, because if we regard iniquity in our hearts, the Lord will not hear us (Psalms 66: 18). For this reason, we had better be reconciled with our offenders before we worship God.

Leave there thy gift before the altar, and go thy way; first be reconciled to thy brother, and then come and offer thy gift. (Matthew 5: 24)

In the Old Testament disputes were mainly settled in courts. This kind of settlement presented no danger to parties involved because grudges did not mount to murder. The Lord Jesus is teaching us to settle disputes out of court so that we give as little time as possible to wrath and be saved from murder.

Agree with thine adversary quickly, whiles thou art in the way with him; lest at any time the adversary deliver thee to the judge, and the judge deliver thee to the officer, and thou be cast into prison. Verily I say unto thee, Thou shalt by no means come out thence, till thou hast paid the uttermost farthing. (Matthew 5: 25-26)

When things are dragged through courts, often times feuding parties get separated for good, seeking no forgiveness from each other. In the Old Testament, saints could get away with it, but in the New we cannot, because un-forgiveness takes one to hell. For which reason, Paul said to the Ephesians:

Let all bitterness, and wrath, and anger, and clamour, and evil speaking, be put away from you, with all malice: And be ye kind one to another, tenderhearted, forgiving one another, even as God for Christ's sake hath forgiven you. (Ephesians 4: 31-32)

Murder, being one of the sins that defiles, opens those that are involved in it to activities of evil spirits. The cause of a lot of the troubles in the lives of the un-forgiving is bitterness. Most of the people seeking deliverance from powers of evil would be instantly set free if they forgave their offenders.

IMMORALITY

In the Old Covenant one was guilty of adultery if he (or she) committed it literally. In the New Testament, however, adultery is expanded to include lustful thoughts in the heart.

> *Ye have heard that it was said by them of old time, Thou shalt not commit adultery: But I say unto you, That whosoever looketh on a woman to lust after her hath committed adultery with her already in his heart.* (Matthew 5: 27-26)

The act of adultery is already committed in the heart of one who looks with lust on someone of the opposite sex. By this standard, who can say he (or she) has never committed adultery or fornication in his (or her) heart? We thank God that He forgives our transgressions and buries them into the depth of the sea.

Defiling most of God's people is not literal adultery, but that of the heart. We must recognise the fact that the enemy is working hard at it through incitement to lust. All age groups, without exception, are his target every second of the day. This being the case, careful consideration of what we watch, or touch is a must. In Matthew 5: 29-30, the Lord Jesus says:

> *And if thy right eye offend thee, pluck it out, and cast it from thee: for it is profitable for thee that one of thy members should perish, and not that thy whole body should be cast into hell. And if thy right hand offend thee, cut it off, and cast it from thee: for it is profitable for thee that one of thy members should perish, and not that thy whole body should be cast into hell.*

If we do not take heed to keep watch by bringing our bodies into subjection, we'll end up into destruction in hell. In dealing with the flesh, we have to be shrewd, setting no unclean thing before our eyes, for instance. David said:

> *I will behave myself wisely in a perfect way. O when wilt thou come unto me? I will walk within my house with a perfect heart. will set no wicked thing before mine eyes: I hate the work of them that turn aside; it shall not cleave to me.* (Psalms 101: 2-3)

Paul too understood the importance of being shrewd with the flesh. He recognised that despite the fact that he preached, he could perish because of the works of his own flesh. He, therefore, brought his body into subjection.

> *I therefore so run, not as uncertainly; so fight I, not as one that beateth the air: But I keep under my body, and bring* it *into subjection: lest that by any means, when I have preached to others, I myself should be a castaway.* (I Corinthians 9: 26-27)

What is confronting us concerning this is huge. Lust is in the air, almost in everything we see and hear. Unless we take an aggressive stand against it, it will take us to hell. By the grace of God, we can walk in victory over lustful thoughts.

FORSWEARING

To forswear is to reject or deny something upon an oath. This practice is forbidden in both the Old and New Covenants (Exodus 20: 7, Leviticus 19: 12, Matthew 5: 33). The Lord Jesus, in His teaching to His disciples, forbids them from both forswearing and swearing.

> *Again, ye have heard that it hath been said by them of old time, Thou shalt not forswear thyself, but shalt perform unto the Lord thine oaths:*

But I say unto you, Swear not at all; neither by heaven;
for it is God's throne: Nor by the earth; for it is his footstool:
neither by Jerusalem; for it is the city of the great King.
Neither shalt thou swear by thy head, because thou canst
not make one hair white or black. (Matthew 5: 33-36)

Because no man is without fault, there cannot lack sin in forswearing. Firstly, the reason for rejecting something upon an oath lies in the confidence that one will never receive or do it. How can mortal man commit himself to such an oath, when present within him is a corrupted nature that can lead him to fall? Most people who say they will never do certain things end up doing the very things they said they wouldn't. The scripture teaches that he who thinks he stands should watch out lest he fall (I Corinthians 10: 12). The power to overcome is not in us, but in the grace God gives.

Secondly, in denial upon oath men claim that they are absolutely truthful in their account of whatever took place. Only God is truthful in everything He says, not mortal man. Whatever happens or causes a dispute involves both sides. Even in the world this is recognised in the saying, "It takes two to tango".

However innocent we may think we are, we cannot be certain, one hundred percent, that we are without fault in a dispute. For instance, our own response to an offence can contribute to the aggravation of the situation. Would we not put ourselves in danger by pleading not guilty upon an oath in such a situation? We must be warned that swearing falsely upon any oath at all is perjury.

The fearful thing is that in forswearing the name of the Lord is profaned (Leviticus 19: 12). It doesn't matter whether it is done by invoking things of this world—God made them. In all forswearing His name is profaned because He is the judge of the earth (Genesis 18: 25). All judgements upon this earth are delegated to the judiciary to carry on His behalf—If they are passed on false evidences His name is profaned.

In the Old Testament men were allowed to make vows to the Lord. However, we have to be careful to note that the scripture warned time and again that delay or failure in honouring the vows would have consequences. In Ecclesiastes 5: 4-5 and Deuteronomy 23: 21, the Lord said:

> *When thou vowest a vow unto God, defer not to pay it; for* he hath *no pleasure in fools: pay that which thou hast vowed. Better* is it *that thou shouldest not vow, than that thou shouldest vow and not pay.* (Ecclesiastes 5: 4-5)

> *When thou shalt vow a vow unto the LORD thy God, thou shalt not slack to pay it: for the LORD thy God will surely require it of thee; and it would be sin in thee.* (Deuteronomy 23: 21)

God's word does not change. Those that make vows today mustn't delay or falter in keeping them either. Many in the house of God are suffering the consequences of un-honoured vows. They make promises without the faintest idea that faltering on their words would have far reaching consequences. For instance, those that make pledges in offerings, but fail to honour them are not guiltless.

We must refrain from making promises with oaths because we are not without fault. It is possible that we can fail in keeping them one way or the other.

The Lord Jesus teaches us not to swear at all. Invoking of the name of God, or heaven, or earth, or Jerusalem, or even our own head or any other things, we mustn't do. Being truthful is what is required of us in what we say; our yes being yes, and our no being no. In the book of James it is explained that in so doing we are saved from falling into condemnation.

> *But above all things, my brethren, swear not, neither by heaven, neither by earth, neither by any other oath: but let your yea be yea; and your nay, nay; lest ye fall into condemnation.* (James 5: 12)

Where swearing is used to back what is said, it is questionable whether it is true. From the Lord's teaching it is clear that acceptance or denial of anything by answers other than yes or no, proceed from evil (Matthew 5: 37).

REVENGE

Revenge was allowed in the Old Covenant, but in the new it is forbidden. Jesus, speaking:

> *Ye have heard that it hath been said, An eye for an eye, and a tooth for a tooth: But I say unto you, That ye resist not evil: but whosoever shall smite thee on thy right cheek, turn to him the other also.* (Matthew 5: 38-39)

We are not allowed to avenge ourselves, but rather to love our enemies. Love is the strongest weapon in resolving of conflicts. Therefore, when assaulted, we mustn't put up fights. Instead we are to turn the other cheek also to be smitten. If sued for our coats we are not to fight to keep them, but let the prosecutor to take also our cloaks. It is confrontational to force someone into doing something, but even in this we are not to resist. Instead we are required to do double the amount of work we are compelled to do.

GIVING

We are to give all who ask of us and those that would borrow from us we mustn't turn away. Of all conditions for giving this is the hardest. When people realise that someone always gives, some begin to take advantage and abuse the kindness. The Lord does not teach us to stop giving in such circumstances, but to pray for those that despitefully use us.

The gospel according to Luke teaches us to lend and not expect return of the items. Would we not save ourselves a lot of heartaches if we heeded this teaching?

Often borrowed things are never returned. I believe the Lord is teaching us not to expect the things to be returned, to protect our own selves from sinning in grudge. In our expectations of the things we actually robe ourselves of peace. Suffering offence because of things of this world that will pass away? It is not worth it. Moreover grudges can lead to murder!

LOVE

In the Old Testament one is allowed to hate his enemy, but in the New we are to love them instead.

> *Ye have heard that it hath been said, Thou shalt love thy neighbour, and hate thine enemy. But I say unto you, Love your enemies, bless them that curse you, do good to them that hate you, and pray for them which despitefully use you, and persecute you;*

> *That ye may be the children of your Father which is*
> *in heaven: for he maketh his sun to rise on the evil and on*
> *the good, and sendeth rain on the just and on the unjust.*
> (Matthew 5: 43-45)

Love for our enemies is one of the things that separate us from the people of the world, for they love those that love them, and salute only those that salute them.

> *For if ye love them which love you, what reward have ye?*
> *do not even the publicans the same? And if ye salute your*
> *brethren only, what do ye more than others? do not even*
> *the publicans so? Be ye therefore perfect, even as your Father*
> *which is in heaven is perfect.* (Matthew 5: 46-48)

The best weapon in ridding ourselves of bitterness is love for our enemies—It brings instant results. Try it, the joy it'll bring; you'll never find any other way! More importantly, this saves us from hell, for we are forgiven our transgressions as we forgive others their trespasses against us.

In the Old Testament people got away with un-forgiveness because revenge was allowed. For instance, King David did not forgive Shim-e-i, the man from Ba-hu-rim, who cursed him when he was escaping from his son Absalom during the rebellion (II Samuel 19: 15-23, I Kings 2: 8-9)—yet he got away with it. From the word of God we see that David made it to heaven.

In conclusion, more is demanded of New Testament saints than those in the Old because more is given them.

In the Old Testament

- The Law was given God's people on two tablets of stone, and in a book. They had to go to the tabernacle of gathering to listen to the reading of the word of God and had to endeavor to remember it in order to meditate in it day and night. How easy is that?
- They were not given the Holy Ghost to indwell them. Therefore, the works of their own flesh worked to hinder them from keeping the word of God.
- This covenant did not provide a permanent remedy for sin. The high priests, who were themselves imperfect, had to enter into the Holy of Holies twice every year on the tenth day of the seventh month, to make atonement for themselves and their families, for Israel and for the sanctuary.

In the New Testament

- The Law is written on the tablets of the hearts of God's people.
- They are given the Holy Spirit to indwell them to give them power to overcome the old nature (the law of sin and death) within them so that they can keep the Law.

- The New Covenant provides a permanent remedy for sin, for the perfect Lamb of God and High Priest, the Lord Jesus (Yeshua), with His own blood, has made atonement for sin once and for all (Hebrews 10: 9-12).

Clearly, the New Testament was made on better promises than those on which the Old Testament was made.

CHAPTER 7

Almsgiving

The teaching of the Lord concerning almsgiving, deals with our motives for doing them more than anything else.

It is important to understand that almsgiving is a kind of prayer. We see this in what Cornelius, the centurion of the Italian band at Caesarea did. He was devout and feared God with his entire house. Besides praying always to God, he gave much alms to the people. Let us take note that his prayers and almsgiving went together before God for a memorial. The angel of the Lord that was sent to deliver the message to him said:

> *Thy prayers and thine alms are come up for a memorial before God. And now send men to Joppa, and call for one* Simon, *whose surname is Peter: He lodgeth with one Simon a tanner, whose house is by the sea side: he shall tell thee what thou oughtest to do.* (Acts 10: 4-6)

What qualifies or disqualifies our almsgiving before God are the motives in doing them. Wrong motive in almsgiving earns the giver no reward from our heavenly Father. For this reason, the Lord teaches us to pay careful attention when giving alms.

> TAKE heed that ye do not your alms before men, to be seen of them: otherwise ye have no reward of your Father which is in heaven. Therefore when thou doest thine alms, do not sound a trumpet before thee, as the hypocrites do in the synagogues and in the streets, that they may have glory of men. Verily I say unto you, They have their reward. (Matthew 6: 1-2)

The lesson in the above passage is that it is hypocritical to announce or testify of one's alms deeds, be it in the house of God or in the world.

We get greatly tempted to make known our alms deeds to gain appreciation from our fellow men, but we must learn to overcome this. Apart from being rewarded by God, in doing almsgiving in secret we are also saved from pride.

Where it is difficult to keep almsgiving secret is in ourselves, but we must. The Lords teaches that we are not to let our left hand know what the right hand does.

But when thou doest alms, let not thy left hand know what thy right hand doeth: That thine alms may be in secret: and thy Father which seeth in secret himself shall reward thee openly. (Matthew 6: 3-4)

What is there to boast about when present within us is a selfish nature that would otherwise not give, except for the grace that God gives us in overcoming it? Let the fact that it is by the grace of God that we can have something and be able to give, keep us on the humble side. Therefore, we must refrain from boasting of almsgiving, even in ourselves.

CHAPTER 8

Prayers and fasting

Prayer is communication with God, in worship, and to inquire, ask, request, long for, desire, and in proclamation. The Lord Jesus teaches that men ought always to pray and not to faint (Luke 18). This means there is need for all mankind to always pray to God. Firstly, it is because the created being and, indeed, the entire creation have no power in themselves to exist. They have to depend on the Word that made them for sustenance. The book of Hebrews teaches that God is upholding all things by the word of His power (Hebrews 1: 3).

Secondly, if creation had to depend on the Word for existence even in the perfect condition in which it was made, how much more should it depend on the Word in a fallen world?

Moreover, the devil is an adversary of all mankind, to tempt them with the intent that they too end up into damnation in everlasting fire prepared for him and his angels (Matthew 25: 41).

The first Adam fell into his temptation, and consequently the entire humankind. Therefore, there is need for all men to pray to God that they be saved from the damnation of the devil.

Before the Lord Jesus taught His disciples the manner in which they ought to pray, He dealt with hypocrisy in praying. Motive to impress men and legislation are the things that make prayers hypocritical.

Motive to impress men

Wrong motives in praying are due to the works of our own flesh, one of which is in seeking recognition from men. Our prayers are to be made to God, but if they are misguided to impress men, then they are vain. The real motive behind dramatising of prayers is a show of one's spirituality. God is only interested in prayers made from the heart, devoid of fleshly manifestations. Sincerity in praying is, therefore, a must if we are to be accepted by the Lord.

> *And when thou prayest, thou shalt not be as the hypocrites* are: *for they love to pray standing in the synagogues and in the corners of streets, that they may be seen of men. Verily I say unto you, They have their reward.* (Matthew 6: 5)

The temple of the Lord in us can easily become a place of idols through the thoughts of our hearts. We must realise that a multitude of sacrifices are of no purpose before God without sincerity of heart. They are instead abominations to Him (Isaiah 1: 11-15). I believe the reason the Lord Jesus dealt with hypocrisy in praying before teaching us the manner in which we are to pray is because He knows it is our weakness. Would we not consider the ways of our doings and seek cleansing of our sins so that we may offer sacrifices that are acceptable to God? Always remember that we are a holy priesthood called to offer spiritual sacrifices that are acceptable to God by Jesus Christ (I Peter 2: 5).

Praying in secret

The motive to impressing men is mainly injected into praying by awareness that people might be watching us as we pray. As soon as we allow this to happen, we begin drawing to God with our lips when our hearts are focused on making impression on men. The solution to this problem is in praying in secret, the benefits of which are in finding environments in which we can focus our minds solely on God. Such praying takes us into the secret place of the Most High. I believe that if we can be trusted in the secrecy of our own praying, we can also be trusted with the secrets of the Lord.

Even after we have entered into our closets and shut out everyone, the battle is not over yet. What occupies the heart cannot be shut outside the door. If they are people or things of this world, they become idols in our hearts, causing us to draw to God with our lips when our hearts are far from Him.

It is how we deal with our treasures that determine what occupies our hearts and minds.

Where a lot of Christians are losing the battle in this area is in how they spend their time. What most people do not realise is the fact that whatever takes one's time occupies the mind and heart of the person. The scripture demands that we spend all our time on meditating in the word of God.

> *This book of the law shall not depart from thy mouth; but thou shalt meditate therein day and night, that thou mayest observe to do according to all that is written therein: for then thou shalt make thy way prosperous, and then thou shalt have good success.* (Joshua 1: 8)

The mind cannot be idle—The times we fail to meditate in the word of God, our minds are occupied on the things of this world. When we are desirous of things of this world, it is difficult for us to focus on God. For our desires to be for the things of God we have to lay our treasures in heaven, for where they are, there our hearts will be also. To lay our treasures in heaven, we have to surrender all that we have to the kingdom of God.

Legislation

All forms of routine in praying mount to legislation; the most common of which are repetitions. They are a form of legislation because people tend to use them as rules for praying certain ways. Prayer, like devotion, cannot be legislated because God is interested in the heart. The Lord forbids His people from using repetitions in praying because they are vain.

> *But when ye pray, use not vain repetitions, as the heathen* do: *for they think that they shall be heard for their much speaking. Be not ye therefore like unto them: for your Father knoweth what things ye have need of, before ye ask him.* (Matthew 6: 7-8)

Despite the Lord's teaching against repetitions, the very model of prayer that He has given His disciples to pray along has been turned, by many today, into the most subtle form of repetitions in praying. The vast majority of people recite it in few minutes without giving it a thought! Some say it repeatedly, thinking that the more they do, the more they are heard of God. It is not in much speaking that we are heard, but in what we say meaningfully to God.

We have to understand that prayers that touch God are those that are from the heart. A few words drawn from the heart are better than many repetitions. There is no need to complicate prayer—it is simply talking to God in worship and about issues that burden our hearts.

THE MANNER IN WHICH WE OUGHT TO PRAY

The right manner in which to approach God is in deep reverence to His name and office. Coming to Him in any other way is not acceptable to Him. Our prayers are to be made to our Father who is in heaven in the following manner:

> After this manner therefore pray ye: Our Father which art in heaven, Hallowed be thy name. Thy kingdom come. Thy will be done in earth, as it is in heaven. Give us this day our daily bread. And forgive us our debts, as we forgive our debtors. And lead us not into temptation, but deliver us from evil: For thine is the kingdom, and the power, and the glory, for ever. Amen. (Matthew 6: 9-13)

In the above passage is given us an outline along which we are to pray making, our petitions known to God in adoration, praise, contrition, supplication and thanksgiving from our hearts. There are other places in scripture where the Lord commands us to pray; and considering them, we find that they all fit into the model of prayer that the Lord is teaching us above.

God is our Father

We are to begin our prayers by acknowledging that God is our Father who is in heaven. Clearly, this shows that the kingdom of heaven is a family, and we are all inclusive. We understand from the gospel according to John that God, the head of this family, has an only begotten Son, Jesus (Yeshua).

> *For God so loved the world, that he gave his only begotten Son, that whosoever believeth in him should not perish, but have everlasting life.* (John 3: 16)

Yet, the scripture also teaches that the Lord Jesus is the firstborn amongst many brethren.

> *For whom he did foreknow, he also did predestinate* to be *conformed to the image of his Son, that he might be the firstborn among many brethren.* (Romans 8: 29)

The fact that the Lord Jesus Christ is God's only begotten Son means that His brethren are sons of God by adoption. The book of Romans teaches us how believers in the Lord Jesus become adopted sons of God.

> *For as many as are led by the Spirit of God, they are the sons of God. For ye have not received the spirit of bondage again to fear; but ye have received the Spirit of adoption,*

> *whereby we cry, Abba, Father. The Spirit itself beareth witness with our spirit, that we are the children of God: And if children, then heirs; heirs of God, and joint-heirs with Christ; if so be that we suffer with* him, *that we may be also glorified together.* (Romans 8: 14-17)

The seal of adoption into the family of God is by the Holy Ghost whom He has given us. The Spirit of God bears witness within us that we are sons of God. How? When we receive the Lord Jesus, the Holy Ghost begins work to transform us into the likeness of Christ, if we are willing to yield to Him.

> *But as many as receive him, to them gave he power to become the sons of God,* even *to them that believe on his name:* (John 1: 12)

Power is present in everyone that has received the Lord, to enable them to surrender their own wills so that they may be made into the sons of God. How they are made into sons of God is by obeying His Spirit, for as many as are led by the Spirit of God, they are the sons of God.

If we fail to understand that the kingdom of God is a family, we'll be in danger of missing His will. Because of misconception of the structure of the kingdom today, many are busy building their own kingdoms using the name of He, who alone, owns the kingdom! The sad thing is, they are not even aware that they are headed to destruction.

Why it is important to understand that the kingdom of heaven is the family of God is so that we may learn to revere Him for His office and His holy name—as well as learn to keep the family values of His kingdom. In a family it is required that;

1. Respect is given the head of the family (the father). This is for his office in carrying the responsibilities for the family, and for fatherhood in the home. In most families children, in respect, do not call their parents by their names. The names commonly used for fathers are Daddy, Dad, Papa, and so on. For mothers the names commonly used are Momma, Mommy, Mom and others.

Notice that in the Ten Commandments, after the commands by which we are to relate to God (our heavenly Father), the next is the one by which we are to relate to our earthly parents. It reads:

> *Honour thy father and thy mother: that thy days may be long upon the land which the LORD thy God giveth thee.*
> (Exodus 20: 12)

Children who are not taught to respect and honour their parents find it difficult to revere and honour God. Because there is hardly any respect for fatherhood in many families today, there is also no respect for the heavenly Fatherhood (God)—The consequences of which are apparent in the lives of many today. Clearly, it is a cursed generation!

2. The brotherly covenant within the family mustn't be broken. The bond that ties a family together is in the blood of the fatherhood. All the children of a man have a common blood flowing through them, that is, the blood of their father. It is important that the brotherly relationship (covenant) be kept in peace between all the children.

There are consequences if this covenant is broken. For instance, the descendants of Esau, and those of Lot were and are still being punished today for not keeping peace with Israel. They didn't care, and their descendants are still not caring today that they have a common blood flowing in them. Edom and Amalek descended from Esau the brother of Jacob, while Ammon and Moab descended from Lot, the nephew of Abraham. The descendants Esau were even more severely punished because they were/are the closest relations of Israel and yet they had and their descendants still have perpetual hatred for her.

> *Thus saith the LORD; For three transgressions of Edom, and for four, I will not turn away the punishment thereof; because he did pursue his brother with the sword, and did cast off all pity, and his anger did tear perpetually, and he kept his wrath for ever: But I will send a fire*

upon Teman, which shall devour the palaces of Bozrah.
(Amos 1: 11-12)

The lesson we are to learn here is that the body of Christ is a family. The blood that is binding us together in brotherly covenant is that of the Father through the Lord Jesus Christ. That is why we must endeavour to keep the unity of the Spirit in the bond of peace to one another.

With all lowliness and meekness, with longsuffering, forbearing one another in love; Endeavouring to keep the unity of the Spirit in the bond of peace. (Ephesians 4: 2-3)

Those, within the kingdom, that are contentious and divide the body are severely punished. We must fearfully learn from the eleventh chapter of I Corinthians and be warned that those who failed to discern the body of the Lord were weak, sick and some even died! (I Corinthians 11: 17-34).

Another area where many in the house of God are bringing curses upon themselves is in their attitude towards Israel. The fact remains that we are joined together with her in a brotherly covenant. Therefore, if we do not maintain the bond of love in peace with her, we'll suffer the consequences.

We mustn't hate or envy Israel's position and prosperity because she is God's firstborn (Exodus 4: 22). The Law stipulates that the firstborn be given double of everything (Deuteronomy 21: 17). Apostle Paul said that Israel has advantage over gentiles in practically every way. Chiefly, because to them were committed the oracles of God.

> *What advantage then hath the Jew? or what profit* is there *of circumcision? Much every way: chiefly, because that unto them were committed the oracles of God.* (Romans 3: 1-2)

To be against Israel includes scorn and resentment of her prosperity. One of the reasons many gentile churches are hurting today is because of their scorning of Israel for keeping of the Law and God's appointed feasts, including the Sabbath. This is a self inflicted wound. They would be healed of it if they repented of their ways and kept the bond of love in peace with their elder brother, Israel.

Outsiders that sow discord amongst brothers are also punished. In the book of Amos we see that one of the reasons for the punishment of Tyre was because they delivered up the children of captivity to Edomites who had joined themselves to Babylonians against Judah, in the days of calamity of Jerusalem.

> *Thus saith the LORD; For three transgressions of Tyrus, and for four, I will not turn away* the punishment *thereof;*

> *because they delivered up the whole captivity to Edom,*
> *and remembered not the brotherly covenant:* (Amos 1: 9)

The book of Proverbs teaches that there are six things that the Lord hates, and seven that are abominations to Him. One of the things is a false witness, and he that sows discord among brethren (Proverbs 6: 19).

God extended His heavenly kingdom onto the earth through the family of Adam, whom He made perfect after His likeness. It was not until the fall that the perfect family that God placed on the earth was corrupted. Since then the devil's war has been and still is centred on attacking of family units to break them. The perfection of family that the first Adam lost has been restored in the last Adam (Jesus). He, with His own blood, has now made all things new concerning the family of the kingdom of God.

> There is *one body, and one Spirit, even as ye are called in*
> *one hope of your calling; One Lord, one faith, one baptism,*
> *One God and Father of all, who* is *above all, and through*
> *all, and in you all.* (Ephesians 4: 4-6)

Clearly, what is crucial in our understanding of the kingdom of heaven is the Fatherhood. God is the head of this family to which we all belong. Therefore, it is required of us that we honour Him for His office, and revere His holy name—as well as maintain the brotherly covenant with every member of the kingdom.

God's name is to be hallowed

God's name is to be hallowed on earth as it is in heaven. This does not only mean deep respect of the phonetic sound of His name, but includes how we conduct ourselves daily before Him and in the world. Because we are His, in sinning we profane His holy name. Psalms 23: 3 teaches that He leads us onto the paths of righteousness for His own name's sake.

God will not hold guiltless those that take His name lightly (Exodus 20: 7). Yet many are today invoking His name as if He is their equal! Some of the ways some people use God's name are so blasphemous that they cannot even dare to use the names of their fellow men! What makes this generation to think that there are no consequences for using God's name as a swear word? In Old Testament times if someone cursed the name of the Lord, he was taken outside the city and stoned to death.

> *An thou shalt speak unto the children of Israel, saying, Whosoever curseth his God shall bear his sin. And he that blasphemeth the name of the LORD, he shall surely be put to death,* and *all the congregation shall certainly stone him: as well the stranger, as he that is born in the land, when he blasphemeth the name* of the LORD, *shall be put to death.* (Leviticus 24: 15-16)

Because God is long-suffering, men are today daring to shake their fists at Him. Let them wait, for it won't be long before His judgements become dramatic in these last days! This is not a threat. We can all read it for ourselves in the Book of Revelation, so that our hearts may learn to fear Him.

God's name is holy

In Heaven God's name is continually being held in deep respect in recognition of His holiness. We see this in the sixth chapter of the book of Isaiah as it was revealed to him (Isaiah) by the six winged seraphim that cried one to another, saying:

> . . . *Holy, holy, holy, is the LORD of hosts: the whole earth is filled with his glory.* (Isaiah 6: 3)

The only way we can approach God is in holiness. Because all men, without exception, have fallen short of the glory of God, there is need for us to seek cleansing as we come before Him. The psalmist recognised this fact and said:

> *Who shall ascend into the hill of the LORD? or who shall stand in his holy place? He that hath clean hands, and a pure heart; who hath not lifted up his soul unto vanity, nor sworn deceitfully. He shall receive the blessing from the LORD, and righteousness from the God of his salvation.*

This is *the generation of them that seek him, that seek thy face, O Jacob. Selah.* (Psalms 24: 3-6)

The generations of them that seek God are, and have always been those who, through repentance, are cleansed of their transgressions. Only in brokenness can we truly repent, and when we do, God is faithful to forgive and cleanse us of our sins.

If we confess our sins, he is faithful and just to forgive us our sins, and to cleanse us from all unrighteousness. (I John 1: 9)

We thank God for Christ's death on Golgotha, for His blood makes a way for us to come boldly to the throne of grace (Hebrews 4: 16). Because of the cleansing of the blood of the Lamb we can approach God and call on His holy name.

God's name represents His nature and office

God is to be revered for His nature and office. From generation to generation, this is expected of all the inhabitants of the earth, as is commanded them in the everlasting gospel.

And I saw another angel fly in the midst of heaven, having the everlasting gospel to preach unto them that dwell on the earth, and to every nation, and kindred, and tongue, and people, Saying with a loud voice, Fear God, and give glory to him; for the hour of his judgment is come: and worship him that made heaven, and earth, and the sea, and the fountains of waters. (Revelation 14: 6-7)

God requires that men fear and worship only Him, firstly because He judges unrighteousness and secondly, because of His works.

Fearing God for His judgements

One of the reasons why we must hate evil is because God judges unrighteousness. Fear of the judgements of God is so important that He made one of the missions of His Spirit on earth to be conviction of mankind of the fact that the consequence of unrighteousness is damnation in hell. The Lord Jesus, speaking:

Nevertheless I tell you the truth; It is expedient for you that I go away: for if I go not away, the Comforter will not come unto you; but if I depart, I will send him unto you. And when he is come, he will reprove the world of sin, and of righteousness, and of judgment: Of sin, because they believe not on me; Of righteousness, because I go to my Father, and ye see me no more; Of judgment, because the prince of this world is judged. (John 16: 8-11)

The Holy Ghost is given to reprove us of our sins so that we may be saved from the damnation of the devil. Hell was not made for man, but for the devil and his angels. However, if we continue in sin, we'll end up in the same place.

How sad it is that many in the world and in the house of God have chosen to go against the convictions of the Spirit and are, therefore, not afraid of the judgements of God.

- In the world this is evident in the jokes of many that it will be more fun to be in hell! When they shall be faced the reality of hell in the end, they will think otherwise, but the sad thing is, it will be too late.
- In the house of God, lack of fear of His judgments is evident in the rebellion of many against His commandments. When they are rejected in the end for being workers of iniquity (lawless), it will be too late (Matthew 7: 21-23).

It is for each one of us to answer if we are trembling at God's word. The fear of the Lord is in hating evil. Unless we learn to fear God's judgements, we'll continue in stubbornness just like a child that doesn't fear punishment keeps on disobeying his parents. This being the case, isn't it a wonder that many preachers are today not teaching about hell? If the people are not made to be aware of the judgement that awaits the disobedient in hell, how will they learn to fear the judgements of God?

Clearly, these are troublesome times. The people that Paul said would in the last days do the things that he named below, that are clearly works of the flesh, have a form of godliness. This means they are people that claim to be of the household of God.

> *This know also, that in the last days perilous times shall come. For men shall be lovers of their own selves, covetous, boasters, proud, blasphemers, disobedient to parents, unthankful, unholy, Without natural affection, trucebreakers, false accusers, incontinent, fierce, despisers of those that are good, Traitors, heady, highminded, lovers of pleasures more than lovers of God; Having a form of godliness, but denying the power thereof: from such turn away.* (II Timothy 3: 1-5)

The denial of the power of godliness in the lives of the people described above is in their refusal to surrender to God's will. This kind of stubbornness is the evidence of the lack of fear of God's judgements in their lives.

In a father-son relationship it is the father that sets the terms and conditions of the relationship. We have to recognise that God is the Father and, therefore, Master in our relation with Him. The only way we can relate with Him is in holiness because He is holy.

The Ten Commandments are the foundation upon which lives, structures of families and nations are to be built. Therefore, we must fear and hate sin because there are consequences for disobeying God.

Revering God for His works

God is to be revered for His works because unfathomable are the depths of His wisdom and understanding. Visibly they are displayed in the works of His hands.

> *The heavens declare the glory of God; and the firmament sheweth his handywork. Day unto day uttereth speech, and night unto night sheweth knowledge.* There is *no speech nor language,* where *their voice is not heard. Their line is gone out through all the earth, and their words to the end of the world. In them hath he set a tabernacle for the sun, Which* is *as a bridegroom coming out of his chamber,* and *rejoiceth as a strong man to run a race. His going forth* is *from the end of the heaven, and his circuit unto the ends of it: and there is nothing hid from the heat thereof.*
> (Psalms 19: 1-6)

There is no nation under the heavens that has been left without witness of the existence of God. In all we see in creation, we are to be awe-struck at the wisdom and understanding of God. They are past our finding in that it can take us the whole of our lifetimes to study any one of His creations and still fail to learn all about it. Surely, the Creator of the universe deserves to be worshiped.

God has, through His works, revealed more about His name and glory to those in covenant relationship with Him. Examples:

1. The Lord revealed Himself as a deliverer when He brought the children of Israel out of Egypt. The ever living God "I AM THAT IAM—THE LORD" is His warring name. He revealed it to Moses when He sent him to confront the then Pharaoh to let Israel go out of Egypt. One of the things Moses declared in his song after they had crossed the Red Sea was, *The LORD* is *a man of war, the LORD* is *his name* (Exodus 15: 3).

2. God revealed Himself as a banner for His people when He defeated the Amalekites in the wilderness. Moses built an altar and called its name THE LORD OUR BANNER—YHVH NIS-SI (Exodus 17: 15).

3. The Lord revealed Himself as the provider for His people when He provided Abraham a ram to be offered for a sacrifice instead of Isaac. Abraham called the name of the place of the altar on Mount Moriah, YHVH JI-REH (Genesis 22: 13-14).

Honouring God in the way we receive Him

Revering God for His office also means honouring Him in the way we receive Him. It is required that children stand up to receive their fathers and the elderly. Showing God our Father respect in this way can be when reading His word, or worshiping Him in prayers and with music. Throughout the scriptures we see how saints reverenced the presence of the Lord. Examples:

-   When God was giving the Ten Commandments, the children of Israel stood and trembled as He spoke (Exodus 20: 21).
-   For the reading of God's word the children of Israel stood up, sometimes for hours! For instance, in Nehemiah 8: 10 we see that when Ezra opened the book of the Law, all the people stood up for the reading. From morning until midday he read from the book—and all the while the people wept as they understood how they had not kept the commandments of the Lord (Nehemiah 8: 3).
-   When saints encountered the glory of God's presence they fell flat on their faces. For instance, Ezekiel, when he say the glory of the God of Israel (Ezekiel 1: 28).
-   In turning back to God, the children of Israel repented of their transgressions in sackcloth and ashes.

Some people might take such actions as outdated, but let us wake up to the fact that they add up. Of course showing such actions in hypocrisy mounts to nothing. However, postures that show humility help in denying the self-centred nature in the flesh, making supplicants more receptive to the things of God.

In contrast, today many seem to approach God as if He is their equal! They have no reverence for His word or authority, let alone the lack of fear of His holy name. If in the natural it is required that we rise up before our parents, elders, and rulers, how much more respect should we give God Almighty?

> *Thou shalt rise up before the hoary head, and honour the face of the old man, and fear thy God: I* am *the LORD.*
> (Leviticus 19: 32)

In the scripture are examples of individuals and generations that have been blessed for honouring their parents, the elderly or those in authority. If God blesses those that honour earthly authorities, how much more will He bless those that honour Him?

Thy kingdom come

We are to pray that God's kingdom come so that His will may be done on earth as it is in heaven. Concerning this, we have to be careful not to focus only on our own selves and our loved ones, or nations. The big picture concerning this is in God's plan or purpose for the earth, for His will is that it be perfect and replenished by man, whom He has given dominion over everything on it. If we understand this, we won't be content with this present world, but seek God's kingdom and His will to be done on the earth. Since this will come about as a result of the liberation of the sons of God, everyone of us should be in prayers with groaning, longing to be restored to the perfect condition in which man was made, spirit, soul and body.

For we know that the whole creation groaneth and travaileth in pain together until now. And not only they, but ourselves also, which have the firstfruits of the Spirit, even we ourselves groan within ourselves, waiting for the adoption, to wit, *the redemption of our body.* (Romans 8: 22-23)

God's kingdom being His domain, by praying His kingdom come and His will be done in the earth; we seek Him to reign in the entire world. In the beginning God's kingdom was on the earth and His will was done on it as it is in heaven. Adam and Eve walked in submission to the will of God until the day they fell at the tree of the knowledge of good and evil.

Man caused the problem because of his sin. In the salvation of the sons of God shall be the liberation of the entire creation.

In the end the kingdoms of this world shall become our Lord's, and of His Christ; and He shall reign forever and ever (Revelation 11: 15). Isaiah prophesied that in that time the earth shall be full of the knowledge of the glory of the LORD, just as the waters cover the sea (Isaiah 11: 9).

Therefore, we mustn't think we have attained where are in right now. Our forefather Abraham, despite the fact that he was righteous and had all things pertaining to life, did not rest, but looked for a city which had foundations, whose builder and maker is God (11: 10). In other words, Abraham longed for the time when God's kingdom would be established on the earth—for His tabernacle (the New Jerusalem) shall descend from Him onto the earth (new earth), and He shall dwell in the midst of His people (Revelation 21).

Give us this day our daily bread

In asking God for our daily bread we acknowledge our dependency on Him. Our daily bread includes food and the word of God. If we direct our efforts mainly on seeking earthly bread, we'll neglect the need for the true bread that came to us from heaven. Man does not live by bread alone, but by every word that proceeds out of the mouth of God (Deuteronomy 8: 3).

In the wilderness God balanced the need for earthly bread and that of heavenly bread in the lives of the children of Israel by causing them to hunger.

> *And he humbled thee, and suffered thee to hunger, and fed thee with manna, which thou knewest not, neither did thy fathers know; that he might make thee know that man doth not live by bread only, but by every* word *that proceedeth out of the mouth of the LORD doth man live.*
> (Deuteronomy 8: 3)

Uncontrolled appetite fights against hunger and thirst for righteousness. It is the reason why they that love their bellies aren't able to endure the suffering of the cross (Philippians 3: 18-19). Hunger is included amongst the things that we are to suffer for the sake of the gospel. The Lord causes us to hunger for the same reason He caused the children of Israel to hunger in the wilderness. It is to teach us to focus our energy on seeking the knowledge of God, rather than on food that perishes.

In John chapter six it is recorded how the Lord Jesus Christ taught the multitude that followed Him, explaining to them the need for seeking bread that never perishes. They, however, continued to seek Him to feed them like their forefathers were fed with manna in the wilderness. Nevertheless, the Lord Jesus continued to teach them that His purpose was not to give them bread that perishes, but that He was the bread of life that came down from heaven.

When the Lord told them to eat His body and drink His blood so that they would have eternal life, they were offended. At that point many left Him, including some of His disciples, to the point that He was left with the twelve only.

Things have not changed. Today many go to the house of God to seek what they expect Him to do for them; and sadly, in most cases they are earthly things that they seek after. This is evident in the popular prosperity messages of these days. Meetings that focus on seeking spiritual food are poorly attended! Yet, seeking of the knowledge of God is of uttermost importance in the life of every child of God.

Even people in the world know that bread alone is not enough for man. They find this out by the emptiness that is in their hearts. This emptiness was put in man by God, and only He can fill it.

Because the world does not know that man is to live by every word that proceeds from the mouth of God, they try to fill the void with things like alcohol, drugs, smoking and other things, but to no avail. It is understandable if people in the world do not seek the knowledge of God, because they are lost. The question is, why the lack of hunger and thirst for righteousness in the house of God?

Forgive us our sins

In repentance, we are to pray God to forgive us our sins. However, we are forgiven only as we forgive others their trespasses against us. Concerning this the Lord teaches that the kingdom of heaven is like a certain king which would take account of his servants. He commanded that the one that owed him ten thousand talents be sold with his wife and children and all that he had, to pay his debt. The servant fell on his face and pleaded with his lord to have mercy and be patient with him, for he would pay all. His lord had compassion on him and loosed him and also forgave him the debt.

The servant, who had just been forgiven, on the contrary, would not forgive his fellow servant that owed him 100 pence. He went out and got hold of him and demanded that he pay all his debt. The debtor pleaded with him to give him more time to pay, but he wouldn't show him mercy. He cast him in prison till he would pay him the debt he owed. When the deeds of this unforgiving servant was reported to his master, he threw him in prison for not being compassionate towards his fellow servant (Matthew 18: 23-34). The Lord Jesus concludes this parable by saying:

> *So likewise shall my heavenly Father do also unto you, if ye from your hearts forgive not every one his brother their trespasses.* (Matthew 18: 35)

Clearly, debt of 100 pence is nowhere close to ten thousand talents in amount. This parable opens our eyes to see that we owed the Lord much more than our fellow men have or ever will owe us. The price the Lord Jesus paid for our transgressions is much more than the debts our fellow men owe in their sins against us. God forgives our transgressions because of His mercy on us. It is, therefore, required that we also forgive those that sin against us, daily, from our hearts.

Offences are inevitable because we live in a fallen world. Nevertheless, it doesn't matter how many times we are offended in a day, we have to forgive. The Lord Jesus' answer to Peter, when he asked Him how many times he was to forgive his brother, was:

> *. . . I say unto thee, Until seven times: but, Until seventy times seven.* (Matthew 18: 22)

This means we are to forgive even if someone offends us 490 times in a day! Yet, sadly, many people hold grudges over offences that were committed against them only once. If God dealt with us thus over every offence that we make against His Law, how many of us would stand? The psalmist fearfully recognised this fact and said:

> *If thou, LORD, shouldest mark iniquities, O Lord, who shall stand?* (Psalms 130: 3)

If we are grateful that God forgives us our transgressions and does not remember them, we must do the same to our fellow men that transgress against us.

Lead us not into temptation

This is a prayer (plea) in seeking God not to give us up to our own ways (lusts), and the temptations of the evil one. God does not lead anyone into temptation.

> *Let no man say when he is tempted, I am tempted of God: for God cannot be tempted with evil, neither tempteth he any man: But every man is tempted, when he is drawn away of his own lust, and enticed. Then when lust hath*

conceived, it bringeth forth sin: and sin, when it is finished, bringeth forth death. (James 1: 13-15)

In light of the above scripture we learn that we are tempted when we are drawn away by our own lusts. However, God can give up individuals or nations to their own ways or evil, if they, in stubbornness, continue to disobey His voice. The multitudes that He will give up to believe the lie in these last days are such. In II Thessalonians 2: 9-12, we read:

Even him, *whose coming is after the working of Satan with all power and signs and lying wonders, And with all deceivableness of unrighteousness in them that perish; because they received not the love of the truth, that they might be saved. And for this cause God shall send them strong delusion, that they should believe a lie: That they all might be damned who believed not the truth, but had pleasure in unrighteousness.*

How many people, who profess to be children of God, are today breaking the Ten Commandments at will? Moreover, leaders of many congregations are lifting commandments of men above the word of God, and the people love to have it so! The time will come, in these last days, when God will send strong delusions on such people that they may believe the lie.

We must be warned that it is the responsibility of every believer in Christ to follow only leadership that are submissive to the word of God. Let's beware of the fact that today many leaders are particularly opposed to the Law and the prophets. From such we must flee.

There is hope for individuals or nations as long as God continues to chastise and punish them for their sins. It means they are sons (Hebrews 12: 8). When He gives up on anyone or a nation, it means they are no longer His. Therefore, we must pray to God to give us hearts of flesh that we may not be stubborn to His voice.

Deliver us from evil

Because sin entered into the world, there is need for men to pray without fainting (ceasing) that they may be vindicated against their adversary the devil. There is a case against us all. The accusation is of sin and we are guilty, for all men have fallen short of the glory of God. Therefore, there is need for us to be justified if we are to escape damnation in hell.

Men, being dead in their transgressions, need a redeemer to save them from damnation. God's plan of redemption of mankind was not a reaction to the fall in the Garden of Eden. The Lamb of God was slain from the foundation of the world (Revelation 13: 8). God promised that the seed of the woman would bruise the serpent's head, and he, His heel (Genesis 3: 15). The seed came through the lineage of Seth to Abraham, through Isaac's son, Israel from whom descended David. He, the Messiah, is known as the Son of David, even the Lord Jesus Christ.

The Judge of the earth will always do right

God, the Judge of the earth, will always do right. The only way He can justify us is if we repent of our sins and seek forgiveness from Him. When righteousness is imparted us, our adversary can have no case to accuse us of sin. For example, he could not find a case against Job because he was righteous.

> *There was a man in the land of Uz, whose name* was *Job; and that man was perfect and upright, and one that feared God, and eschewed evil.* (Job 1: 1)

Job feared God to the point that he daily offered also scarifies for sin on behalf of his children.

> *And it was so, when the days of* their *feasting were gone about, that Job sent and sanctified them, and rose up early in the morning, and offered burnt offerings according to the number of them all: for Job said, It may be that my sons have sinned, and cursed God in their hearts. Thus did Job continually.* (Job 1: 5)

Job was righteous, not because of his works, but because he continually sought God for forgiveness of his transgressions. We, likewise, are justified and therefore, saved from damnation in hell if we remain broken and contrite before the Lord.

The question is, can we be vindicated of the Lord against our adversary the devil like Job was? The day the sons of God presented themselves before Him, the devil also amongst them, He asked the adversary if he had considered Job.

> *And the LORD said unto Satan, Hast thou considered my servant Job, that* there is *none like him in the earth, a perfect and an upright man, one that feareth God, and escheweth evil?* (Job 1: 8)

Anyone of whom the Lord can give such a testimony is blessed indeed. Contrition and brokenness of spirit is the way to attain such a testimony. King David recognised this and said:

> *For thou desirest not sacrifice; else would I give* it: *thou delightest not in burnt offering. The sacrifices of God* are a *broken spirit: a broken and a contrite heart, O God, thou wilt not despise.* (Psalms 51: 16-17)

The reason why most people cannot be justified (declared guiltless) is because of the hardness of their hearts. It is a fact that most people in the house of the Lord today are not far from the state that the children of Judah were in before the Babylonian captivity. God told Jeremiah that their hearts were so hard that they had engraved their sins upon them with a pen of iron, with the pint of diamond!

> *The sin of Judah* is *written with a pen of iron,* and *with the point of a diamond:* it is *graven upon the table of their heart, and upon the horns of your altars;* (Jeremiah 17: 1)

The Lord had called them to go back to the old paths, wherein was the good way, so that they would have rest for their souls, but they refused. He then set watchmen over them to warn them of judgement that was looming, but they refused to hearken to the sound of the trumpet (Jeremiah 6: 16-17). The Lord had warned them, rising up early, but they would not turn back to Him. He had sent His prophets to them, rising up early to warn them, but they would not turn back.

How far is this generation from where Judah was? Despite the fact that judgement is looming, today most people in the house of God are adamantly going their own ways! The call to them to turn back and walk according to the commandments of the Lord, they flatly reject. In so doing, they by themselves are making it impossible for God vindicate them against their adversary the devil.

We mustn't faint in seeking repentance

We cannot afford to faint in prayer of repentance. The Lord Jesus has given a parable to teach men to be persistent in seeking to be delivered from the snares of the devil.

> *And he spake a parable unto them* to this end, *that men ought always to pray, and not to faint; Saying, There was in a city a judge, which feared not God, neither regarded man: And there was a widow in that city; and she came unto him, saying, Avenge me of mine adversary. And he would not for a while: but afterward he said within himself, Though I fear not God, nor regard man; Yet because this widow troubleth me, I will avenge her, lest by her continual coming she weary me. And the Lord said, Hear what the unjust judge saith. And shall not God avenge his own elect, which cry day and night unto him, though he bear long with them?* (Like 18: 1-8)

Why we have to pray without fainting is because the devil does not rest in his efforts to destroy us. He roams to and fro the face of the earth seeking whom he may devour (I Peter 5: 8). His efforts are in tempting us so that we may remain in unbelief and be not saved from our sins.

Faith is the fuel for persistence in prayer

The Lord concluded the parable in Luke 18: 1-8 by saying, *Nevertheless, when the Son of man cometh, shall he find faith on the earth?* Clearly, prayerlessness is the problem here. Without faith we cannot pray, for he that comes to God must know that HE IS and that He rewards those that seek Him diligently (Hebrews 11: 6). Faith involves personal attachment to God, shown in reliance on Him and commitment to Him. Meaningful and persistent prayers come from hearts that have placed their trust in God.

The Lord has shown us in the parable of the widow and the unjust judge that men faint in seeking deliverance when they take long in forthcoming. Yet, usually it is they by themselves that hinder their deliverance. The hindrances can be as a consequence of the following:

- Due to iniquity in the heart: The psalmist said: If I regard iniquity in my heart, the Lord will not hear *me*: (Psalms 66: 18).
- Because of refusal to obey the Law. Proverbs 28: 9 says: He that turneth away his ear from hearing the law, even his prayer *shall be* abomination.
- Due to estranged heart: From Isaiah 29: 2, we read: Wherefore the Lord said, Forasmuch as this people draw near *me* with their mouth, and with their lips do honour

me, but have removed their heart far from me, and their fear toward me is taught by the precept of men:

- Separation from God due to sin: In Isaiah 59: 1-2, the Lord says: BEHOLD, the LORD's hand is not shortened, that it cannot save; neither his ear heavy, that it cannot hear: But your iniquities have separated between you and your God, and your sins have hid his face from you, that he will not hear.

- Because of waywardness: Jeremiah 14: 10-12 says: Thus saith the LORD unto this people, Thus have they loved to wander, they have not refrained their feet, therefore the LORD doth not accept them; he will now remember their iniquity, and visit their sins. Then said the LORD unto me, Pray not for this people for *their* good. When they fast, I will not hear their cry; and when they offer burnt offering and an oblation, I will not accept them: but I will consume them by the sword, and by the famine, and by the pestilence.

- Because of offering unworthy sacrifices: In Malachi 1: 7-9, we read: Ye offer polluted bread upon mine altar; and ye say, Wherein have we polluted thee? In that ye say, The table of the LORD *is* contemptible. And if ye offer the blind for sacrifice, *is it* not evil? and if ye offer the lame and sick, *is it* not evil? offer it now unto thy governor; will he be pleased with thee, or accept thy person? saith the LORD of hosts. And now, I pray you, beseech God that he will be gracious unto us: this hath been by your means: will he regard your persons? saith the LORD of hosts.

- Due to hypocrisy: (Matthew 6: 5-6).

- Because of pride and self-righteousness: Luke 18: 11-14 says: The Pharisee stood and prayed thus with himself, God, I thank thee, that I am not as other men *are*, extortioners, unjust, adulterers, or even as this publican. I fast twice in the week, I give tithes of all that I possess. And the publican, standing afar off, would not lift up so much as *his* eyes unto heaven, but smote upon his breast, saying, God be merciful to me a sinner. I tell you, this man went down to his house justified *rather* than the other: for every one that exalteth himself shall be abased; and he that humbleth himself shall be exalted.

- Because of lack of faith: In Hebrews 11: 6, we read: But without faith *it is* impossible to please *him*; for he that commeth to God must believe that he is, and *that* he is a rewarder of them that diligently seek him.

- Because of asking amiss: In James 4: 3 we learn that we can ask, and receive not, because of not asking according to the will of God, but to consume on our own lusts.

- Due to doubt and double mindedness: James 1: 6-8 teaches that he who wavers and is double minded cannot receive anything from the Lord.

If the unjust judge was wearied and vindicated the widow for her persistence, how much more will God deliver from evil His own elect that cry to Him day and night?

Where our sanctification is concerned, we must realise that the delay is not from God's side, but in ourselves. It takes the renewal of our minds for us to be transformed into the likeness of Christ. As for God, His will is that this transformation takes place swiftly in our lives. Should anything that we desire be what can work against our relationship with Him, He will make us suffer delay in receiving them until we are mature enough or denial of them altogether.

Why it is taking us years to deal with our old natures is simply because of not following the way of the Lord. If both baptisms in water and in the Spirit are not being urgently sought after today, how can we deal with the works of the flesh swiftly?

Persistent prayer is Spirit-led. Except the Spirit of God helps our infirmities, we soon dry out and then praying becomes very tedious. On the other hand, Spirit-led praying is so refreshing and has longevity! If we spend our time in praying the kind of prayers that cannot be received by the Lord, the answers will not come and soon we'll faint and quit.

The kingdom

We are to end our prayers by acknowledging that the kingdom, the power and the glory belong to God forever and ever. In this we keep reminding ourselves that we mustn't, at any time, lay claim to anything in the kingdom or the power that is in it and the glory.

Literally, everything the Lord puts in our possession or under our care, we are to steward. King David understood this very well. In his prayers of thanksgiving after he and the princes and the elders of Israel had given abundantly for the building of the temple, he acknowledged that God owned everything they had, including their lives.

> *Wherefore David blessed the LORD before all the congregation: and David said, Blessed be thou, LORD God of Israel our father, for ever and ever. Thine, O LORD, is the greatness, and the power, and the glory, and the victory, and the majesty: for all that is in the heaven and in the earth is thine; thine is the kingdom, O LORD, and thou art exalted as head above all. Both riches and honour come of thee, and thou reignest over all; and in thine hand is power and might; and in thine hand it is to make great, and to give strength unto all.*
>
> *Now therefore, our God, we thank thee, and praise thy glorious name. But who am I, and what is my people, that*

> *we should be able to offer so willingly after this sort? for all*
> *things* come *of thee, and of thine own have we given thee.*
> *For we* are *strangers before thee, and sojourners, as* were
> *all our fathers: our days on the earth* are *as a shadow, and*
> there is *none abiding. O LORD our God, all this store*
> *that we have prepared to build thee an house for thine*
> *holy name* cometh *of thine hand, and* is *all thine own.* (I
> Chronicles 29: 10-16)

David thanked God for enabling them to give to Him, and acknowledged that they had given of His own. We must seek to reach this point in our walk with the Lord, otherwise it will be impossible to find rest in Him.

The greatest bondage in one's live is selfishness. It is a prison, the gate of which is called 'self'. Sadly, most people in the house of God are unaware that they are in this prison, and yet they are suffering its effect. In John 8: 36, we read: *If the Son therefore shall make you free, ye shall be free indeed.*

Most people think that this is freedom from attacks of the enemy, but it isn't. It is rather, freedom from the corruption that plagued the soul of man at the fall in the Garden of Eden. One of the corruptions was selfishness that became a nature in the soul. True freedom is in conquering self. Therefore, those that would be free have to consider all that is in their possession not their own, but God's. Those that reach this point get heavy weights of burden lifted off their shoulders and are, therefore, free indeed. Such people give and share things freely, without any pain! That is real freedom!

The early church understood their position very well. They recognised that the kingdom of God is a family and, therefore, surrendered all in their possession to be had in common.

> *And all that believed were together, and had all things common; And sold their possessions and goods, and parted them to all* men, *as every man had need.* (Acts 3: 44-45)

> *And the multitude of them that believed were of one heart and of one soul: neither said any* of them *that ought of the things which he possessed was his own; but they had all things common. And with great power gave the apostles witness of the resurrection of the Lord Jesus: and great grace was upon them all.*
>
> *Neither was there any among them that lacked: for as many as were possessors of lands or houses sold them, and brought the prices of the things that were sold, And laid* them *down at the apostles' feet: and distribution was made unto every man according as he had need.* (Acts 4: 32-35)

We had better mean it when we call Jesus Lord. The title "lord" means "owner". Those that fail to surrender all to Him may call

Him, Lord, Lord, the way they like, they will remain workers of iniquity (Matthew 7: 21-23).

John the Baptist prepared the way of the Lord, making His paths straight by dealing with self-centredness. He preached a blazing message that hit at the heart of the strongest thing that is holding man, self.

> *Then said he to the multitude that came forth to be baptized of him, O generation of vipers, who hath warned you to flee from the wrath to come? Bring forth therefore fruits worthy of repentance, and begin not to say within yourselves, We have Abraham to our father: for I say unto you, That God is able of these stones to raise up children unto Abraham. And now also the axe is laid unto the root of the trees: every tree therefore which bringeth not forth good fruit is hewn down, and cast into the fire.*
>
> *And the people asked him, saying, What shall we do then? He answereth and saith unto them, He that hath two coats, let him impart to him that hath none; and he that hath meat, let him do likewise.*
>
> *Then came also publicans to be baptized, and said unto him, Master, what shall we do? And he said unto them, Exact no more than that which is appointed you. And the soldiers likewise demanded of him, saying, And what shall we do? And he said unto them, Do violence to*

*no man, neither accuse any falsely; and be content with
your wages. (Luke 3: 7-14)*

It is important for us to take note of the fact that John called
the whole multitude a generation (brood) of vipers. This clearly
shows that they were a multitude of people who were not yet
converted. For them to be truly converted, he had to contend
with self-centeredness in their lives.

Today, what is hurting the gospel more than anything else is
selfishness. The mentalities of many of those calling on the name
of the Lord seem to be—God for us all, but every man for himself!
The consequences of which are self inflicted. The Church would
experience revival if all believers in the Lord Jesus Christ became
selfless.

The power and the glory

The power and the glory in the kingdom belong exclusively to
God. Those that try to claim them soon dry out, for God will
not give His glory to another (Isaiah 42: 8, 48: 11). He entrusts
with the power of Pentecost only those that acknowledge that the
kingdom, the power and the glory are His. Where we must be
warned is when He works signs and wonders through us. There
is a great temptation to begin thinking that God works through
one because he (or she) is anointed!

We had better keep on the humble side. Christ is "The Anointed One". This means none of us is—The anointing that we operate in is flowing down to us from the head (Christ). It is like oil that was poured on Aaron's head that flowed down to his beard, and down his garments to his feet.

> *Behold, how good and how pleasant* it is *for brethren to dwell together in unity!* It is *like the precious ointment upon the head, that ran down upon the beard,* even *Aaron's beard: that went down to the skirts of his garments; As the dew of Hermon,* and as the dew *that descended upon the mountains of Zion: for there the LORD commanded the blessing,* even *life for evermore.* (Psalms 133)

Advertisement of miracles and signs does not glorify God, but the minister. In this way, many are touching the glory that belongs exclusively to God, and are, therefore, polluting His holy name. In Isaiah 48: 10-11, the Lord says:

> *Behold, I have refined thee, but not with silver; I have chosen thee in the furnace of affliction. For mine own sake,* even *for mine own sake, will I do it: for how should* my name *be polluted? and I will not give my glory unto another.*

In light of the above scripture, we see that the reason God chooses us in the furnace of affliction is to keep us humble that we may not profane His holy name by touching His glory.

The Lord Jesus would not allow any publication of the works that were done through His hands. He told everyone He healed not to tell anybody, except the demoniac of Gadara (Mark 5: 1-20). Probably the reason the Lord told him to go back into his country and declare what things God did for him, was because the people of that coast had asked Him to leave the area. The Lord probably sent him to his own people as a witness. Later when returning from the coast of Tyre to Galilee, He passed through Decapolis (Mark 7: 31), which was the very area from which He was asked to depart after He had delivered the possessed man.

It is meaningless, as well as hypocritical, to end prayers declaring, *Thine is the kingdom, the power and the glory, for ever and ever*, without surrendering to God. Let us be warned that all hypocrites shall not inherit the kingdom of heaven.

FASTING

In the Sermon on the Mount the Lord's teaching concerning the subject of fasting focuses particularly on the motive to impress people with it.

> *Moreover when ye fast, be not, as the hypocrites, of a sad*
> *countenance: for they disfigure their faces, that they may*
> *appear unto men to fast. Verily I say unto you, They have*
> *their reward.* (Matthew 6: 16)

The purpose of fasting is to afflict the soul so that one can soar in the things of God. It is, therefore, hypocritical if our motive in fasting is to impress people of our spirituality. At the end of the day, it is God's opinion that matters. Earning praise of our fellow men for fasting is an utter waste of time.

CHAPTER 9

No one can serve two masters

What determines where our services are dedicated is our love, for we are servants to whomever we love. We are either serving God or mammon, depending on whether our love is set on God or on worldly riches.

> *No man can serve two masters: for either he will hate the one, and love the other, or else he will hold the one, and despise the other. Ye cannot serve God and mam-mon.* (Matthew 6: 24)

Our works are acceptable to God only if they are from our hearts. Rivalling our love for God are our treasures because they are tied to our hearts and cannot be separated. For this reason the Lord teaches us to beware of where we lay them.

> *Lay not up for yourselves treasures upon earth, where moth and rust doth corrupt, and where thieves break through and*

steal: But lay up for yourselves treasures in heaven, where neither moth nor rust doth corrupt, and where thieves do not break through nor steal: For where your treasure is, there will your heart be also. (Matthew 6: 19-21)

Why we mustn't lay our treasures on earth is that our hearts be not on earthly things. If we lay them in heaven, our hearts will be on heavenly things.

How to lay our treasure in heaven

In Luke 18: 18-25 the Lord Jesus has shown us how to lay our treasures in heaven. In this account, the Lord told the rich man to sell all he had and distribute to the poor, and then he would have treasures in heaven. Clearly, it is by giving that we lay our treasures in heaven. Proverbs 19: 17 teaches that he who shows pity on the poor and meets their needs lends to God.

Although it is by giving that we lay our treasures in heaven, love is the condition that qualifies our works to make them to be acceptable to God. Paul recognised this fact and said of acts of kindness:

And though I bestow all my goods to feed the poor, *and though I give my body to be burned, and have not charity, it profiteth me nothing.* (I Corinthians 13: 3)

Many give to good causes, but their treasures are not laid in heaven! The reason being, love is not the motive behind their acts. Selfishness can only be defeated by giving in love.

It is by doing acts of kindness that our treasures are laid in heaven. Commands that God has given His people to remember the cause of the poor like: They are to remember the poor, strangers, widows and the fatherless by not gleaning their harvests (Leviticus 19: 10)-They are not to harvest crops from land that they leave fallow every Sabbath year (Exodus 23: 11)-They are to share their bread with the hungry (Deuteronomy 15: 11, Isaiah 58: 7)—are all acts of love to the needy.

God commands us to give everything we have, not to harm us, but that we may be saved from self-centredness. Love for worldly riches goes at the expense of the salvation of the soul. The only way we can come after the Lord, is if we deny ourselves.

> *Then said Jesus unto his disciples, If any man will come after me, let him deny himself, and take up his cross, and follow me. For whosoever will save his life shall lose it: and whosoever will lose his life for my sake shall find it. For what is a man profited, if he shall gain the whole world, and lose his own soul? or what shall a man give in exchange for his soul? For the Son of man shall come in the glory of his Father with his angels; and then he shall reward every man according to his works.* (Matthew 16: 24-27)

Denial of self is in becoming selfless. It is not until we overcome self-centredness that our hearts are made free of love for the things of this world. When we reach this point, then and only then can we set our love on God and, therefore, be able to serve Him.

The side most of us are failing to see is the fact that giving actually benefits the giver the most. The Lord Jesus said that it is more blessed to give than to receive (Acts 20: 35).

Take no thought for your life

Worry of the future is the reason most people hoard things instead of sharing with the poor and needy. Hoarding actually reveals a lack of faith in the provisions of the Lord for each day. The Lord Jesus teaches us not to even take thought of the future, but to take one day at a time.

> *Therefore I say unto you, Take no thought for your life, what ye shall eat, or what ye shall drink; nor yet for your body, what ye shall put on. Is not the life more than meat, and the body than raiment? Behold the fowls of the air: for they sow not, neither do they reap, nor gather into barns; yet your heavenly Father feedeth them. Are ye not much better than they?*
>
> *Which of you by taking thought can add one cubit unto his stature? And why take ye thought for raiment? Consider*

the lilies of the field, how they grow; they toil not, neither do they spin: And yet I say unto you, That even Solomon in all his glory was not arrayed like one of these.

Wherefore, if God so clothe the grass of the field, which to day is, and to morrow is cast into the oven, shall he *not much more* clothe *you, O ye of little faith? Therefore take no thought, saying, What shall we eat? or, What shall we drink? or, Wherewithal shall we be clothed?*

(For after all these things do the Gentiles seek:) for your heavenly Father knoweth that ye have need of all these things. But seek ye first the kingdom of God, and his righteousness; and all these things shall be added unto you. Take therefore no thought for the morrow: for the morrow shall take thought for the things of itself. Sufficient unto the day is the evil thereof. (Matthew 6: 25-34)

We must learn to trust God for provision, one day at a time. He renews His mercies every morning. This means the grace He gives is to take us through each day. Therefore, there is no point in trying to solve the problems of tomorrow on the mercies of today. We have to trust God for the future. His mercies have never failed. Tomorrow He will be there for us—next week He will be there for us—next year He will be there for us—in ten years time He will be there for us. God is always there—He inhabits eternity.

CHAPTER 10

Judgement and condemnation

The Lord Jesus commands us to judge not, that ye be not judged. To judge in this context is to pronounce one doomed to destruction. This must be left to the Lord because He alone knows the hearts of men and judges everyone according to their works. The book of James teaches that he, who condemns another, condemns his Maker.

> *Speak not evil one of another, brethren. He that speaketh evil of his brother, and judgeth his brother, speaketh evil of the law, and judgeth the law: but if thou judge the law, thou art not a doer of the law, but a judge.* (James 4: 11)

We've not been made executors of the judgement of the Law—that belongs to God. From Matthew 7: 1-5 it is clear why we mustn't judge. Simply, it is because none of us is without fault. How can we, who in ourselves cannot keep the righteousness of the Law, judge another? The huge responsibility is on us to deal with our own faults before we can even attempt to see those in others.

> *JUDGE not, that ye be not judged. For with what judgement ye judge, ye shall be judged: and with what measure ye mete, it shall be measured to you again. And why beholdest thou the mote in thy brother's eye, but considerest not the beam that is in your own eye? Or how wilt thou say to thy brother, Let me pull out the mote out of thine eye; and, behold, a beam is in thine own eye? Thou hypocrite, first cast out the beam out of thine own eye; and then shalt thou see clearly to cast out the mote out of thy brother's eye.* (Matthew 7: 1-5)

The Lord has shown us that our faults are much greater than those that we see in others—They are like beams compared to those in others which are but like tiny specks. This is the fact to which the Lord Jesus drew the attentions of those that wanted to stone the woman who was caught in adultery (John 8: 3-11).

By telling them that he who had no sin should be the one to cast the first stone, the Lord convicted the accusers of the woman of their own transgressions, which must have been a lot greater than the sin of the accused. Sure enough, they all went away one by one, leaving only the woman with Jesus. The Lord having not come to this world to condemn, but to save, let the woman go, telling her not to sin anymore.

Furthermore, judgement must be left to God because of the following reasons:

1. God is just.

God is just in all His judgements, but men aren't. The injustice we see in the world, both now and in the time past, are evidences of man's incapability in judgement. Take for instance, the case of the adulterous woman in the eighth chapter of John's gospel, if she was caught in the very act of adultery, where was the man with whom she sinned? Surely, there was a bias or partiality in the judgement of the accusers of the woman. According to the Law of Moses both the woman and the man with whom she committed the adultery were to be stoned (Leviticus 20: 10).

A parallel to judgements of our days are those of the days of Isaiah. Judgement had been so corrupted that it was turned backwards. Isaiah described it, saying:

> *And judgement is turned away backward, and justice standeth a far off: for truth is fallen in the street, and equity cannot enter. Yea, truth faileth; and he that departeth from evil maketh himself a prey: and the LORD saw* it, *and it displeased him that* there was *no judgement.*
> (Isaiah 59: 14-15)

The judiciary system described above favoured those that were corrupt, but penalised those that departed from evil. How far is this from our days? If rights of criminals can be put above those of victims, then judgement is turned backward. Surely, truth has also fallen on our streets.

2. In judgement God remembers mercy.

The Lord remembers mercy in judgement. In mercy, He stops short judgements, and sometimes withholds His wrath all together when He sees the suffering of the people. For instance, because of His compassion on Israel, He did not pour out His wrath entirely on her in the wilderness. He remembered that they were flesh and frail.

> *When he slew them, then they sought him: and they returned and inquired early after God. And they remembered that God was their rock, and the high God their redeemer. Nevertheless they did flatter him with their mouth, and they lied unto him with their tongues. For their heart was not right with him, neither were they steadfast in his covenant.*
>
> *But he, being full of compassion, forgave their iniquity, and destroyed them not: yea, many a time turned he his anger away, and did not stir up all his wrath. For he remembered that they were but flesh, a wind that passeth away, and cometh not again.* (Psalms 78: 34-39)

Another instance is in the case of King Ahab. Because he humbled himself and repented, the Lord delayed His judgement on him for killing Naboath the Jezreelite to the days of his son.

> *And it came to pass, when Ahab heard those words* (the Judgement)*, that he rent his clothes, and put sackcloth upon his flesh, and fasted, and lay in sackcloth, and went softly. And the word of the LORD came to Elijah the Tishbite, saying, Seest thou how Ahab humbleth himself before me? because he humbleth himself before me, I will not bring the evil in his days:* but *in his son's days will I bring the evil upon his house* (I Kings 21: 27-29).

Men, on the other hand, show no mercy in executing punishment on wrong doers however much they repent.

3.   Only God can rightly determine judgement.

Only God can determine the extent to which individuals or nations should be punished. For instance, by the time Jerusalem fell to the Babylonians, God had, in His mercy, decided that the punishment of Judah was enough. We see this in His rebuke of the Edomites, wherein He said:

> *Because thou hast had a perpetual hatred, and hast shed* the blood of *the children of Israel by force of the sword in*

the time of their calamity, in the time that their *iniquity* had *an end.* (Ezekiel 35: 5)

Clearly, the punishments for the iniquity of Israel had reached an end in the sight of the Lord. However, the Babylonians, joined by the children of Edom, carried on to destroy Jerusalem and the temple of the Lord and took Judah into captivity.

When men judge, they go all the way till someone pays the ultimate penalty, but God remembers mercy. That was why when Israel was to be judged because King David had counted the people; the king chose to fall into the hands of God rather than man.

> *And the Lord spake unto Gad, David's seer, saying, Go and tell David, saying, Thus saith the LORD, I offer thee three* things: *choose thee one of them, that I may do* it *unto thee.*
>
> *So Gad came to David, and said unto him, Thus saith the LORD, Choose thee Either three years' famine; or three months to be destroyed before thy foes, while that the sword of thine enemies overtaketh thee; or else three days the sword of the LORD, even the pestilence, in the Land, and the angel of the LORD destroying throughout all the costs of Israel.*
>
> *Now therefore advise thyself what word I shall bring again to him that sent me. And David said unto Gad, I am in a great strait: let me fall now into the hand of the*

LORD; for very great are *his mercies: but let me not fall into the hand of man.* (I Chronicles 21: 9-13)

When the angel that the Lord sent to Jerusalem went about destroying the city, God remembered mercy and commanded the angel, saying, . . . *It is enough, stay now thine hand* . . . (I Chronicles 21: 15).

4. God is long-suffering.

God takes long before He judges, giving transgressors time to repent of their ways. For example, we read in the book of Jeremiah that over the centuries He warned the children of Israel, giving them time to turn back to Him.

- God sent His servants many times warning them, because He had compassion on them and on His dwelling place (Jeremiah 7: 25; 25: 3, 4; 35: 15; 44: 4; 29: 19; 26: 5).
- God spoke to them, rising up early (Jeremiah 7: 13; 11: 7; 35: 14).

No nation or individuals have been judged without warning because God does not delight in the destruction of the wicked. For instance, those that were destroyed by flood in the time of Noah were warned for 969 years that judgement was coming. We know this from the accounts of the lives of Methuselah, and his grandson Noah.

The name Methuselah was prophetic, giving the people warning that when he (Methuselah) died, judgement would come. Methuselah means—"his death shall bring". The evidence of the warning in this name is clearly seen in the effect it had on his father, Enoch. After he begat Methuselah, the scripture says he (Enoch) walked with the Lord to the point that the He (the Lord) took him.

Genesis 5: 27 teaches that Methuselah lived 969 years and died. Sure enough, the year he died the flood came. We can find this out in the following way:

- Methuselah lived 187 years and begat Lamech.
- Lamech lived 182 years and begat Noah.
- When Noah was 600 years old, the flood came.

To find out the time from the day Methuselah was born to the flood, we add 187+182+600=969 years. God gave Methuselah the longest life on the face of this earth, in mercy, because his name prophetically carried a warning to the people that perished in the flood. All through Methuselah's lifetime, that is, for 969 years God gave that generation time to turn away from wickedness.

The case of Sodom and Gomorrah is not any different. True, Lot did not preach to Sodom, but he was an example to them of a righteous life. The scripture says that he sat at the gate and grieved over the sins of Sodom.

> *And turning the cities of Sodom and Gomorrha into ashes*
> *condemned* them *with an overthrow, making* them *an*
> *ensample unto those that after should live ungodly; And*
> *delivered just Lot, vexed with the filthy conversation of the*
> *wicked: (For that righteous man dwelling among them, in*
> *seeing and hearing, vexed* his *righteous soul from day to*
> *day with* their *unlawful deeds;)* (II Peter 2: 6-8)

At the gates of Sodom were the rulers thereof seated from day to day running the affairs of the city. Surely, Lot sitting amongst them and grieving over the sins of the city was enough warning to them that God punishes unrighteousness.

5. God's wrath works righteousness in those that repent, but that of man does not.

> *For the wrath of man worketh not righteousness of God.*
> (James 1: 20)

Wrath of man leads to manifestations of the works of the flesh in the lives of feuding parties; such manifestations as bitterness, revenge, hatred, murder, resentment, withdrawal and others.

Discipline mustn't be turned into judgement

We have to be careful not to carry on with discipline to the point that what was meant to be corrective turns into judgement and condemnation. The goal of discipline is to restore, not to condemn. One of the signs that disciplinary actions have turned into judgement and condemnation is when the repentant person is denied the opportunity to function in his (or her) place in Christ. Who are we to render such a one not fit for ministry?

We have to remember always that the gifts and calling of God are without repentance (Romans 11: 29). God alone decides when one is no longer of the kingdom. He turns round the lives of those who repent. Therefore, the repentant should be allowed to continue with their ministry.

It is sad that some believers have had their ministries terminated by leadership that decided to consider them unfit after they had fallen into sin! If God dealt with all of us thus, sincerely, how many of us would still be in ministry today?

Repentance being a heart issue, we can never tell when someone who is to be judged or one who is under judgement repents. If we are not careful, we'll be in danger of punishing or wishing punishment on people who have already repented and have been forgiven in the sight of the Lord. For example, the prodigal son repented and put himself right with God and his father, but his elder brother thought it was not appropriate to celebrate his return, still holding his sins against him, saying,

> *... Lo, these many years do I serve thee, neither transgressed*
> *I at any time thy commandment: and yet thou never gavest*
> *me a kid, that I might make merry with my friends: But*
> *as soon as this thy son was come, which hath devoured thy*
> *living with harlots, thou hast killed for him the fatted calf.*
> (Luke 15: 29-30)

We all have to watch our attitude towards the prodigals lest we become judgemental. Those that stigmatise prodigals for their sins of the past must be warned that it is un-forgiveness and, therefore, their own sins will not be forgiven either. Furthermore, self-righteousness, doggedness, loveless nature, jealousy, pride, hypocrisy; are revealed in the lives of those that bar prodigals from coming back into the house of God. People with such dispositions cannot inherit the kingdom of heaven.

Paul wrote to the Corinthian church, in II Corinthians 2: 5-11, to show mercy and receive back the adulterous man whom he had said earlier should be punished (I Corinthians 5). This was, firstly, to keep their disciplinary actions to corrective measures. Secondly, it was to stop the devil from taking advantage of both the church and the man that sinned, in destroying them.

Judge not, that you be not judged

If we judge, the same measure of judgement shall be returned to us when it is pressed down, shaken together and running over. In Luke 6: 37-38, we read:

> *Judge not, and ye shall not be judged: condemn not, and ye shall not be condemned: forgive, and ye shall be forgiven: Give, and it shall be given unto you; good measure, pressed down, and shaken together, and running over, shall men give into your bosom. For with the same measure that ye mete withal it shall be measured to you again.*

What happened to the children of Edom are examples to us of such greater measures of judgement that are returned to those that judge. They joined the Babylonians in destroying Jerusalem, saying . . . *Rase it, rase it, even to the very foundation thereof* (Psalms 137: 7). In this, they encouraged their ally to completely wipe off the city. Also it is revealed in the book of Obadiah that the children of Edom put up the road block at which Zedekiah with his sons and the princes of Judah were captured.

> *Neither shouldest thou have stood in the crossway, to cut off those of his that did escape; neither shouldest thou have delivered up those of his that did remain in the day of distress.* (Obadiah 1: 14)

193

It is important to take note that what the Edomites wanted done to Israel happened to them instead, to a greater extent than they wished for Israel. Their desire was for Israel to be erased that she be no more a nation, but it is Edom that is not a nation today, without any clear trace of exactly who their descendants are!

CHAPTER 11

Cast not your pearls before the swine

The Lord Jesus teaches us not to give what is holy to dogs nor cast our pearls before the swine. There are people who have no intention of seeking truth, but come to try to draw us into arguments and endless genealogies, to the end that they might damage our faith. From such we must turn away because they are dangerous.

> *Give not that which is holy unto the dogs, neither cast*
> *ye your pearls before swine, lest they trample them under*
> *their feet, and turn again and rend you.* (Matthew 7: 6)

The Lord shows us that scoffers are intent on trampling the precious word of truth underfoot and rending us (ripping our faiths to bits)! We must be wise not to engage with such people into conversation of any sort.

Also in the epistles we are charged not to strive about words that are unprofitable lest we be subverted.

- Vain and profane babblings we must shun because they increase unrighteousness (II Timothy 2: 14, 16, 23).
- Listening to fables (lies) and genealogies, that give rise to questions rather than godly edification which come about by faith, we must avoid (I Timothy 1: 4).
- Foolish questions, genealogies, contentions, and strivings **about the Law** we must avoid because they are unprofitable and vain.

But avoid foolish questions, and genealogies, and contentions, and strivings about the law; for they are unprofitable and vain. A man that is an heretick after the first and second admonition reject; Knowing that he that is such is subverted, and sinneth, being condemned of himself. (Titus 3: 9-11)

The Law is God's instruction to His people in righteousness. Therefore, there is nothing to argue about it.

- After admonishing heretics twice, if they won't listen, we are not to keep company with them.

Included amongst the things we are to avoid in order to keep the word of faith that is entrusted to us is also opposition of science.

Paul told Timothy that some had erred concerning the faith because of it (I Timothy 6: 20-21). If opposition of science was dangerous to the faith of those that believed in the Lord then, how much more today when knowledge has increased in the world? It will be wise of us to draw a line and not engage into argument of any sort concerning science.

It is about time scientists who are trying to discredit creation left the Bible alone. Science does not prove the word of God. The word of God proves science where there are facts in it. Otherwise the rest of it is foolishness (I Corinthians 3: 19), the evidence of which is in the denial of creation. It can only be esteemed as a vessel of pottery that turns round to say to the potter that he did not make it.

> *Surely your turning of things upside down shall be esteemed as the potter's clay: for shall the work say of him that made it, He made me not? or shall the thing framed say of him that framed it, He had no understanding?* (Isaiah 29: 16)

Clearly, it is a fool that denies the existence and the wisdom of the Creator of the universe (Psalms 53: 1). Precious saints, take heed for it is never wise to argue with a fool. The gospel is to be believed, not argued about. We must, therefore, zealously guard against giving what is holy (the word of faith) to those that want to desecrate it.

Besides, we have a pearl of a great price. It is our union with the Lord Jesus Christ. To bring us salvation, it cost Him His life. We also have to surrender all, including our lives, to be united with Him. This is not something we can afford to cast before to those that are intent on destroying our faith.

CHAPTER 12

Ask, seek and knock

Asking and seeking are ways of desiring something, while knocking on a door is a desire to be received. The Lord Jesus is teaching us to have the confidence that God gives good gifts to those that desire them from Him, and He receives those that desire to come to Him.

> *Ask, and it shall be given you; seek, and ye shall find; knock, and it shall be opened unto you: For every one that asketh receiveth; and he that seeketh findeth; and to him that knocketh it shall be opened. Or what man is there of you, whom if his son ask bread, will he give him a stone? Or if he ask a fish, will he give him a serpent? If ye then, being evil, know how to give good gifts unto your children, how much more shall your Father which is in heaven give good things to them that ask him?* (Matthew 7: 7-11)

In asking we receive, seeking we find and knocking the door is opened to us.

Why we must ask

Although God provides for almost all our needs without us asking Him, there are things for which we have to ask before He can give them to us. This is because in asking is also accountability for the items sought after. There are some things God will not give us except we accept to be accountable for them. For instance, if we ask our parents for our inheritances we have to accept the responsibility for them. This is required of us not to penalise us, but to teach us to acknowledge our transgressions and repent when we have not been faithful with what He gives us.

The prodigal son understood his position very well after he had squandered the inheritance that his father gave him. He knew that he could no longer expect his father to take charge of him. In this, he understood that he was chargeable for the inheritance that he wasted. So, he came back to his father desiring to be received, not as a son, but as one of the hired servants.

The difference between the prodigal son and his elder brother was he asked his father for what belonged to him, while his elder brother didn't (Luke 15: 11-32). There is no point complaining of not receiving from God when the reason is because of not asking. All that God has is ours through the Lord Jesus Christ. If we ask Him according to His will, He will give us.

Why we must seek

Seeking is to desire something by searching. Why we must seek God is so that we may cultivate love in our hearts for Him. We cannot take time to seek Him if we do not have strong desire for Him. From the psalmists of Israel we see how strong desire for God in their lives caused some of them to keep awake in the night so that they could meditate on the word of God—pant for God like the hart pants for the water brooks—long to know the way of His commandments.

The Lord says to His people, *Seek ye my face.* May we answer like David did in his heart, saying . . . *Thy face, O Lord, will I seek* (Psalms 27: 8).

Because King David understood the importance of seeking after God, he went and brought the Ark to him, and put it into the tent that he had prepared for it in the City of David. After he had brought the Ark, he urged all Israel to seek the Lord and His strength continually (I Chronicles 16: 11).

In Proverbs 2:1-9, we are taught of the Lord that if we search for Him like men search for silver and for hidden treasures, then we shall find the knowledge of God.

Why we must knock

The reason for knocking is that we may be received by our Father in heaven. The way to knock that we be received by the Lord is through repentance, for it is the only way we can approach His throne. Therefore, repentance has to be a continual process in our lives through brokenness and contrition.

The first thing one who is received is offered, is usually a seat, otherwise it means the person is not welcome. The Lord sits in a high and lofty place with him that is broken in spirit and has a contrite heart.

> For thus saith the high and lofty One that inhabiteth eternity, whose name is Holy; I dwell in the high and holy place, with him also that is of a contrite and humble spirit, to revive the spirit of the humble, and to revive the heart of the contrite ones. (Isaiah 57: 15)

In repentance we are reawakened to follow after righteousness. Peter told the men that marvelled at the healing of the lame man that always sat begging at the Beautiful gate, to repent so that they could be revived.

Repent ye therefore, and be converted, that your sins may be blotted out, when the times of refreshing shall come from the presence of the Lord; (Acts 3: 19)

Refreshing comes to us from the presence of the Lord. Therefore, it is important that we knock so that we may be received into His presence.

CHAPTER 13

Love for others

In the commandments of the Lord is conveyed His will for us concerning our attitude to one another. After the commands by which we are to relate to our heavenly Father and our earthly parents, the rest of the commandments are those by which we are to relate to our fellow men. The Lord Jesus reiterates the Law and the prophets to us, saying:

> *Therefore all things whatsoever ye would that men should do to you, do ye even so to them: for this is the law and the prophets.* (Matthew 7: 12)

Whatsoever we would that others do to us is what we are to do to all men. In other words, we are to esteem and have regard for others as we would that others do to us. In so doing we learn to love and, therefore, fulfil the Law and the prophets.

Why we must learn to love others as ourselves is firstly because undeserving as we are, God loves us. It is, therefore, required of us to also love our fellow men unconditionally so that God's love may be perfected in us.

> *Herein is love, not that we loved God, but that he loved us, and sent his Son to be the propitiation for our sins. Beloved, if God so loved us, we ought also to love one another. No man hath seen God at any time. If we love one another, God dwelleth in us, and his love is perfected in us. Hereby know we that we dwell in him, and he in us, because he hath given us of his Spirit.* (I John 4: 10-13)

Secondly, love can be known only in the action it prompts. Our love for God is proven by our love for one another.

> *If a man say, I love God, and hateth his brother, he is a liar: for he that loveth not his brother whom he hath seen, how can he love God whom he hath not seen? And this commandment have we from him, That he who loveth God love his brother also.* (I John 4: 20-21)

Thirdly, our discipleship is also proven by our love for one another.

> *A new commandment I give unto you, That ye love one another; as I have loved you, that ye also love one another.*

> *By this shall all* men *know that ye are my disciples, if ye
> have love one to another.* (John 13: 34-35)

In teaching us to love, the Lord has made it clear that it is important for us to keep the Law and the prophets, for when we abide in love we fulfil the righteousness of the Law.

CHAPTER 14

Entering in at the strait gate

We need to understand right away what it takes to make it though the strait gate into life. The Lord Jesus teaches us to strive to walk the narrow way to this gate because it is not easy. Many are trying to enter in, but will not make it. Clearly, coming into the kingdom is not the end of the matter, but is the beginning of our warfare.

Because of the cross to carry daily on this way, many give up and follow instead, the path of least resistance on the broad way leading to destruction. The disciple that asked the Lord Jesus if there be few that are saved, must have realised the difficulties along the narrow way. The scary thing is in the fact that the many that are trying to make it on it won't be able to.

Then said one unto him, Lord, are there few that be saved?
And he said unto them, Strive to enter in at the strait gate:

for many, I say unto you, will seek to enter in, and shall not be able.

When once the master of the house is risen up, and hath shut to the door, and ye begin to stand without, and to knock at the door, saying, Lord, Lord, open unto us; and he shall answer and say unto you, I know you not whence ye are:

Then shall ye begin to say, We have eaten and drunk in thy presence, and thou hast taught in our streets. But he shall say, I tell you, I know you not whence ye are; depart from me, all ye workers of iniquity. (Luke 13: 23-27)

Enter ye in at the strait gate: for wide is the gate, and broad is the way, that leadeth to destruction, and many there be which go in thereat: Because strait is the gate, and narrow is the way, which leadeth unto life, and few there be that find it. (Matthew 7: 13-14)

Because it is not easy to walk the way into life, it is upon each of us to strive to make it. Of those that are trying to enter in at the strait gate, the many that shall be rejected in the end are people who will have thought that they were of the household of God all along! This means that one can be a church attendee and still perish.

Yet, the vast majority of the people in the house of God today think that they'll enter into heaven, simply because they have received the Lord Jesus Christ. Yes, this is true for someone who receives the Lord at the point of death, like for instance, the thief that was crucified on the right hand of the Lord on Golgotha. The fact is, as long as we remain on this earth for any period of time after we have received the Lord, we are going to have to strive to enter in at the strait gate.

The will of God

The warfare on our hands along the narrow way is all about fulfilling the will of God. Unless we abandon our ways and accept to walk with the Lord, we cannot do His will.

> *Can two walk together, except they be agreed?* (Amos 3: 3)

The mystery of God's will is in the fact that He has purposed to gather together all things in Christ the Messiah in the end of times.

> *Having made known unto us the mystery of his will, according to his good pleasure which he hath purposed in himself: That in the dispensation of the fulness of times he might gather together in one all things in Christ, both which are in heaven, and which are on earth; even in him: In whom also we have obtained an inheritance, being predestinated according to the purpose of him*

who worketh all things after the counsel of his own will:
(Ephesians 1: 9-11)

God works all things according to the counsel of His will. They that won't be found in His will shall be cast into the outer darkness where there is weeping and gnashing of teeth. It is, therefore, important that we understand what it means to do the will of God.

When the multitude asked the Lord what they were to do that they might work the works (do the will) of God, His reply to them was:

This is the work of God, that ye believe on him whom he hath sent (John 6: 29).

The will of God is that we believe on the Messiah, whom He has sent to redeem us. Believing on the Lord includes becoming like Him in all we do, for we are predestined to be conformed to the image of the Son of God (Romans 8: 29).

Fulfilling our purpose in Christ

Fulfilling of our purposes in Christ is a must. The multitude that will be outside knocking to be let in after the door is shut—will be people who will have eaten in the presence of the Lord, prophesied, worked miracles and cast out devils in His name. This means church attendance and even ministry do not guarantee entry into life.

> *Not every one that saith unto me, Lord, Lord, shall enter into the kingdom of heaven; but he that doeth the will of my Father which is in heaven. Many will say to me in that day, Lord, Lord, have we not prophesied in thy name? and in thy name have cast out devils? and in thy name done many wonderful works? And then will I profess unto them, I never knew you: depart from me, ye that work iniquity.* (Matthew 7: 21-23)

The reason why the people that the Lord describes in the scripture above shall be rejected is because they will not have done the will of God.

To do the will of God, we have to keep within the boundaries He has set for us pertaining to life and godliness—which boundaries are the Law and the prophets. Our victory over the flesh, the world and the devil is in observing to do as is written in the book of the Law (Joshua 1: 8).

We must understand that we are able to prove what the will of God is for our lives only if we renew our minds.

> *And be not conformed to this world: but be ye transformed by the renewing of your mind, that ye may prove what*

is *that good, and acceptable, and perfect, will of God.*
(Romans 12: 2)

In this, care is to be taken not to think there are different kinds
of the will of God. The second 'that' in this scripture makes
the subject singular. I have heard people talking of doing the
permissible will of God, and some, the perfect will of God. The
will of God for an individual is one; it is good, acceptable and
perfect before Him. We can, therefore, either be in His will or
out of it.

Why we must renew our minds is because the carnal mind cannot
receive the things of God.

> *But the natural man receiveth not the things of the Spirit*
> *of God: for they are foolishness unto him: neither can*
> *he know* them, *because they are spiritually discerned.*
> (I Corinthians 2: 14)

To renew our minds, we have to receive with meekness the
engrafted word (word that replaces evil thoughts in our minds).

> *Wherefore lay apart all filthiness and superfluity of*
> *naughtiness, and receive with meekness the engrafted*
> *word, which is able to save your souls.* (James 1: 21)

It is the power of the engrafted word that is able to save our souls. Why we have to receive the word with meekness is because the things that are rooted in our minds exalt themselves against the knowledge of God (II Corinthians 10: 5). Unless we humble ourselves and cast them down, they will continue to be hindrances to us in receiving the word.

When our minds are renewed, then and only then, can we be able to prove what the will of God is for our lives.

It is important to understand that our ministry in the kingdom is not by trial and error, neither can we choose where to function. The many that shall be rejected despite having been in the house of God and ministered, are those that will have failed to find their purposes in God. It is ministry that the Lord appoints each of us that is His will for us. Those that are self-styled apostles, prophets, evangelists, pastors and so on are in for a rude awakening in the end, if they do not repent and find their places in the body of Christ and function therein.

The renewal of our minds being what determines whether we find the will of God or not, we must do what it takes to be renewed.

Our purposes are in the mind of our Maker

Just as the purpose of every item is in the mind of the manufacturer, our prophetic purposes are in the mind of God our Maker. Before the fall, the mind of God concerning His creation was not hid from man. That was why Adam was able to name all the beasts of the field and fowls of the air after God created them (Genesis 2: 19). After the fall, however, what is in God's mind concerning His creation became as the words of a book that is sealed. The Lord spoke about it through Prophet Isaiah, saying:

> *And the vision of all is become unto you as the words of a book that is sealed, which* men *deliver to one that is learned, saying, Read this, I pray thee: and he saith, I cannot; for it* is *sealed: And the book is delivered to him that is not learned, saying, Read this, I pray thee: and he saith, I am not learned.* (Isaiah 29: 11-12)

Now to find out the purpose of any of God's creation or His purpose for our lives, we have to seek Him. The learned are not advantaged over the unlearned. Anyone that seeks to know the will of God for His life can find it. We are thankful that what Satan tried to destroy through the first Adam, the Lord has restored to us through the last Adam, Jesus Christ. If we be in Him, we can find out the will of God for our lives.

Zeal

It is not enough to know the will of God for our lives. After we have found it, we've got to go ahead and fulfil it; otherwise we won't enter into the kingdom of heaven.

Zeal is the urge that pushes us to do the will of God. It is birthed into our hearts as a result of strong desires to fulfil our purposes. Strong desires are, in turn, birthed in us through prayer and worship, for it is the Lord who makes us perfect in every good work to do His will (Hebrews 13: 21). The burdens He puts in our hearts concerning the work of the kingdom, we mustn't ignore because they are according to His will for each of us. If we accept to conceive them, strong desire will be birthed in us to fulfil our purposes. The Lord Jesus makes our desire for the things we ask of the Father a condition for receiving them.

> *Therefore I say unto you, What things soever ye desire, when ye pray, believe that ye receive them, and ye shall have them.* (Mark 11: 24)

If we strongly desire to fulfil our purposes, the Lord will hear us and birth in us zeal to do His work.

Beware of other visions

We must hold fast the vision God gives and stray not from it to the left or to the right. We need all the strength we can get because we are going to have to fight on a daily basis to stick with the vision that the Lord gives us.

The devil does not use carnal weapons to destroy a man that has found his purpose, but tries to entice him to either abandon God's calling for another vision, or to receive also other visions to bog him down so that he may not fulfil the will of God. Evidently, many have fallen into the devils trap today in their abandoning of the heavenly calling to embrace other visions. Others have added other visions to the heavenly calling and are, therefore, bogged down and ineffectual in doing the will of God for their lives.

This is not a joking matter; the things we prefer or add to the will of God will cost us eternal life, if we do not repent and forsake them.

Keeping within the will of God

Stretching of a ministry to include areas not assigned mounts to an abuse of the office assumed. Besides, it brings unnecessary troubles which would otherwise be avoided by keeping to the vision given.

We keep to the visions assigned us only if we follow the leading of the Spirit. With all due respect, I would that we learn from what happened to Apostle Paul and be warned of how easy it is to stray from the leading of the Spirit. When we see someone commited to Christ like Paul, at some point, walking beyond the limits of the vision given him, the rest of us should watch out.

When Paul decided to go to Jerusalem at the end of his second missionary journey, the Holy Ghost warned him from city to city not to, but he kept on. When he and his company reached Miletus, he sent for the elders of the church of Ephesus to bid them farewell because he knew that they would not see his face again (Acts 20: 16-38). There, he told the elders that he was bound in his spirit to go to Jerusalem, but in every city, the Holy Ghost warned him that bonds and afflictions awaited him (Acts 20: 22-23). Paul felt bound to go to Jerusalem despite all the warnings of the Holy Ghost because he was not afraid of suffering for the name of the Lord (Acts 20: 24).

Yes, indeed, we suffer for the kingdom, but we are not to go looking for it where the Spirit of God is not leading us. I've heard many preachers commending Paul for going to Jerusalem, calling it a determination! Not so! Plainly, he went against the warning of the Spirit of God, and paid the price for it.

The Holy Spirit gave Paul the same warnings in every city so that he could reconsider his course and be saved unnecessary suffering.

When Paul and his company came to Tyre, they found there some disciples of the Lord and tarried with them seven days. They (the disciples) said to him through the Spirit, not to go to Jerusalem (Acts 21: 4). Despite being told plainly not to, Paul continued on his journey to Jerusalem.

From Tyre they went on to Caesarea, and he and his company stayed in the house of Philip the evangelist [one of the seven chosen to take charge of tables when there was a murmuring in the Church (Acts 6: 5)]. While they were in Caesarea, a prophet by the name Agabus came down from Judea. He took Paul's girdle and bound his own feet and hands with it and said;

> . . . *Thus saith the Holy Ghost, So shall the Jews at Jerusalem bind the man that owneth this girdle, and shall deliver* him *into the hands of the Gentiles.* (Acts 21: 11)

The brethren besought Paul with tears not to go to Jerusalem, but he wouldn't be stopped. When Paul reached Jerusalem, James and the elders received his testimony of ministry amongst gentiles and glorified God. They advised him to purify himself together with four men who had taken vows, and shave their heads and be before the Lord in the temple seven days. When the days were nearly ended, Jews that came from Asia stirred up trouble against Paul (Acts 21: 27-28). They thrust him out of the temple and beat and were going to kill him, but the captain of the guard rescued him.

When Paul was given chance to make his defence before the Jews, he admitted that the Lord Jesus Himself had earlier told him to depart from Jerusalem in haste because his testimony would not be received there; and that He would send him to gentiles.

Paul knew he was called to be an apostle to gentiles (Galatians 2: 7), but his own heart's desire kept drawing him to go and testify in Jerusalem. Because he did not heed the leading of the Spirit this time, he left Jerusalem in chains in the hands of gentiles!

If Paul had obeyed the Spirit of God, he would have gone to Rome a free man and imagine how much more ministry he could have done. Think also of the two years he spent in Caesarea as a prisoner. Had he been free amongst gentiles he could have done much more ministry. Paul would probably have lived much more of his life in freedom if he had concentrated on his work amongst gentiles.

Are we sticking with the heavenly calling? We are not any better than Paul. Where he was tempted we are also being tempted. According to the account in Matthew 7: 21-23) the vast majority of those in the house of God are doing worse. Except they repent and begin to walk in the dead centre of the will of God, they'll perish.

Beware of betrayal by fellow ministers

If the enemy cannot succeed in stopping us from fulfilling your purposes, he will try to entice us to sin against God so that we may fall under judgement. The vessels the devil uses to entice God's servants to do contrary to the commands given them by the Lord, are their fellow ministers! When such ministers see the

Lord using another mightily, they become jealous and work to cause the person to do contrary to the will of God so that he (or she) falls!

We may ask if such ministers are of God. Yes, initially they might have been, but if they do not deal with their carnal natures, they'll be envious of the work of God through other people. Instead of being instruments of righteousness they become those for unrighteousness.

An example of this is in the account of what happened to the prophet that was sent by God from Judah to prophesy against the altar of King Jeroboam, at Bethel. The Lord instructed the prophet what to prophesy against the altar, what he should not do in Bethel and how he should return to Judah.

> *And, behold, there came a man of God out of Judah by the word of the LORD unto Beth-el: and Jeroboam stood by the altar to burn incense. And he cried against the altar in the word of the LORD, and said, O altar, altar, thus saith the LORD; Behold, a child shall be born unto the house of David, Josiah by name; and upon thee shall he offer the priests of the high places that burn incense upon thee, and men's bones shall be burnt upon thee.*
>
> *And he gave a sign the same day, saying, This is the sign which the LORD hath spoken; Behold, the altar shall*

be rent, and the ashes that are *upon it shall be poured out.*
(I Kings 13: 1-3)

When King Jeroboam stretched forth his hand from the altar as he gave command to arrest the prophet, his arm became stiff that he could not pull it back. The altar was rent and the ashes poured from it as the prophet had said. The king pleaded with him to entreat the Lord to restore his arm, and he did. The king then asked the man of God to go home with him and eat and drink, but he would not because the Lord had strictly forbidden him from eating or drinking from Bethel.

So far this servant of God was on track with the mission assigned him. He departed to go back to Judah by another way, as the Lord commanded him (I Kings 13: 10).

Present at the place of the altar were sons of an old prophet in Bethel. They returned home and told their father what the man of God from Judah prophesied against the altar, and what happened after that. The old prophet asked his sons which way the man of God went and they saddled him his ass and he quickly went after the prophet from Judah. He found him sitting under an oak tree and asked if he was the man of God from Judah and he answered that he was. The old prophet then asked him to go back with him to eat bread, and that he would give him a reward!

The prophet from Judah explained to the old man that the Lord forbade him from eating bead or dinking in Bethel (I Kings 13: 16-17).

The old prophet deceived the prophet from Judah by giving him another message that he supposedly received from an angel. That the angel had told him to go and bring the prophet from Judah back to his house to eat and drink water! Sadly, he went back with him to Bethel and ate bread and drank. As they were at table, the word of the Lord came to the old prophet, and he cried to the man of God that came from Judah, saying;

> . . . *Thus saith the LORD, Forasmuch as thou hast disobeyed the mouth of the LORD, and hast not kept the commandment which the LORD thy God commanded thee, But camest back, and hast eaten bread and drunk water in the place, of the which* the LORD *did say to thee, Eat no bread, and drink no water; thy carcase shall not come unto the sepulchre of thy fathers.* (I Kings 13: 21-22)

After the old prophet had made the prophet from Judah to fall, he saddled his ass that he may be on his way back to Judah! As he went, a lion attacked and killed him, but did not eat his flesh or his ass. People that passed by saw the carcase of the prophet and the lion standing by it came and told the people of the city where the old prophet dwelt. Listen to what the latter said:

. . . It is the man of God, who was disobedient unto the word of the LORD: therefore the LORD hath delivered him unto the lion, which hath torn him, and slain him, according to the word of the LORD, which he spake unto him. (I Kings 13: 26)

This is serious; this prophet was brought down by someone who was a minister in the office of prophets! The most probable reason for his deed was jealousy. We must beware of fellow ministers who do not support, but work to counteract our visions. Below are some of the ways we can overcome these subtle enemies of our destinies.

- It is not wise to reveal to anyone, instructions that God gives us for carrying out any assignment.

The prophet from Judah shouldn't have told the king of Israel his reasons for not going with him to eat bread and drink in his house. Neither should he have told the reasons to the old prophet from Bethel.

- Messages that counteract instructions that God gives us, we must reject.

The prophet from Judah should have rejected the message of the old prophet from Bethel because it was contrary to the one the Lord gave him. To convince him, the old prophet told him that he too was a prophet. Even if it is an angel that gives us messages, as long as they contradict instructions we've received from God, we must reject them.

Nehemiah is a good example for us concerning this. When he was told by Shem-ai-ah to go and meet him in the house of God within the temple, to supposedly escape from those who would kill him. He (Nehemiah) refused to go because it was not lawful for anyone who was not a Levite to enter into the temple (Nehemiah 6: 10-13). In his answer to Shem-ai-ah, he said:

> *Should such a man as I flee? and who* is there, *that,* being *as I* am, *would go into the temple to save his life? I will not go in.* (Nehemiah 6: 11)

Nehemiah discerned that the message of Shem-ai-ah was not from God, but was intended to entice him to sin against God's command so that he could fall under judgement.

> *And, lo, I perceived that God had not sent him; but that he pronounced this prophecy against me: for Tobiah and Sanballat had hired him. Therefore* was *he hired, that I should be afraid, and do so, and sin, and* that *they might have* matter *for an evil report, that they might reproach me.* (Nehemiah 6: 12-13)

It is important to take note that Shem-ai-ah was a minister of the house of the Lord. The enemies of Nehemiah used him to try to entice him (Nehemiah) to break God's command concerning the work of the sanctuary, so that he could be destroyed.

- We must beware that the enemy will pursue after us.

The devil will not leave someone who has demolished his stronghold to go in peace. He pursues—therefore, we cannot afford to sit down to rest along the way! The prophet from Judah should have travelled back home in haste. When he stopped to sit under the oak tree, he gave the enemy chance to catch up with him.

- When asked of our identities, we mustn't reveal.

The very people to whom we reveal our identities and missions can turn round to work against us. The prophet from Judah shouldn't have told the old prophet who he was, or what his mission was.

When John was asked who he was, he told the people that he was a voice crying in the wilderness (John 1: 23). This was enough for them to know that he was the messenger before the Lord—The Prophet Isaiah had prophesied so.

The Lord Jesus was time and again asked who He was, but He did not reveal. He left it to the Spirit of God to reveal to whoever He willed. Asked by John, through two of his disciples whom he had sent to inquire of Him if He was the Messiah, the Lord would not plainly say that He was. Instead, He told the disciples of John to go and show him the things that were fulfilled in Him. They were enough for John to discern that He was (is) the Messiah.

> *And it came to pass, when Jesus had made an end of commanding his twelve disciples, he departed thence to teach and to preach in their cities. Now when John had heard in the prison the works of Christ, he sent two of his disciples, And said unto him, Art thou he that should come, or do we look for another? Jesus answered and said unto them, Go and shew John again those things which ye do hear and see: The blind receive their sight, and the lame walk, the lepers are cleansed, and the deaf hear, the dead are raised up, and the poor have the gospel preached to them.* (Matthew 11: 1-5)

There is no need to go about telling people who we are. It is enough to fulfil the works we've been assigned. Besides, in revealing who we are to our fellow ministers, is there not a temptation to do so with the intent that we might be pat on the back? If that be the case, where is the humility in it?

In conclusion, **we must strive** to keep to the will of God, that our Lord and Master find us not sleeping when He returns. The assignments He has given us, we must fulfil, for He will require of us accountability for them.

Take ye heed, watch and pray: for ye know not when the time is. For the Son of man is *as a man taking a far journey, who left his house, and gave authority to his servants, and to every man his work, and commanded the porter to watch. Watch ye therefore: for ye know not when the master of the house cometh, at even, or at midnight, or at the cockcrowing, or in the morning: Lest coming suddenly he find you sleeping. And what I say unto you I say unto all, Watch.* (Mark 13: 33-37)

Blessed is the servant, whom when his Lord returns, shall find faithfully doing what He commanded him.

CHAPTER 15

Building on the Rock

We are built on the rock if we hear the teachings of the Lord and do them. Unless we make the teachings that we have received to be our way of life, they cannot benefit us.

> *Therefore whosoever heareth these sayings of mine, and doeth them, I will liken him unto a wise man, which built his house upon a rock: And the rain descended, and the floods came, and the winds blew, and beat upon that house; and it fell not: for it was founded upon a rock.*
>
> *And every one that heareth these sayings of mine, and doeth them not, shall be likened unto a foolish man, which built his house upon the sand: And the rain descended, and the floods came, and the winds blew, and beat upon that house; and it fell: and great was the fall of it.* (Matthew 7: 28-27)

Those who receive the teachings of the Lord and walk in them are immovable like a house that is built on a rock withstands storms. They can say with Paul, in every situation that faces them, that nothing shall separate them from the love of Christ. Through trials, they are persuaded that they are more than conquerors through Christ (Romans 8: 35-39).

On the other hand, those that receive the word, but do not do them are like a house that is built on sand. When the storms of life come they are not able to withstand, and, therefore, fall.

It is therefore, important that we be not hearers only, but doers of the word of God. Apostle James explained that if we be hearers, but practice not the word, we deceive ourselves.

> *But be ye doers of the word, and not hearers only, deceiving your own selves. For if any be a hearer of the word, and not a doer, he is like unto a man beholding his natural face in a glass: For he beholdeth himself, and goeth his way, and straightway forgetteth what manner of man he was. But whoso looketh into the perfect law of liberty, and continueth* therein, *he being not a forgetful hearer, but a doer of the work, this man shall be blessed in his deed.* (James 1: 22-25)

How we learn to be doers of the word is revealed to us in the book of Joshua in chapter 1: 8:

This book of the law shall not depart out of thy mouth; but thou shalt meditate therein day and night, that thou mayest observe to do according to all that is written therein: for then thou shalt make thy way prosperous, and then thou shalt have good success. (Joshua 1: 8)

It is by meditating in the word of God day and night that we can be able to walk according to all that is written in the scripture (be doers of the word). For the sake of the name of the Lord and our eternal souls, may we take heed to walk according to His word. Amen.

Conclusion

In conclusion; it is important to recognize that the Lord is giving us His teachings with authority, and therefore, be diligent in obeying them. The multitude of people that heard them in the beginning of His ministry was astonished, but not many of them persevered to continue with Him on this way.

And it came to pass, when Jesus had ended these sayings, the people were astonished at his doctrine: For he taught them as one *having authority, and not as the scribes.* (Matthew 7: 28-29)

The rock of revelation that the Lord Jesus Christ is the Messiah is given us not just to be marveled at, but to change our lives into His image. Even so, pray we all be found built upon the Rock of Ages. AMEN.

Personal Notes